The Observers' Pocket Series

SHIPS

The Observer Books

A POCKET REFERENCE SERIES COVERING A
WIDE RANGE OF SUBJECTS

Natural History
BIRDS
BIRDS' EGGS
BUTTERFLIES
LARGER MOTHS
COMMON INSECTS
WILD ANIMALS
ZOO ANIMALS
WILD FLOWERS
GARDEN FLOWERS
FLOWERING TREES
      AND SHRUBS
HOUSE PLANTS
CACTI
TREES
GRASSES
FERNS
COMMON FUNGI
LICHENS
POND LIFE
FRESHWATER FISHES
SEA FISHES
SEA AND SEASHORE
GEOLOGY
ASTRONOMY
WEATHER
CATS
DOGS
HORSES AND PONIES

Transport
AIRCRAFT
AUTOMOBILES
COMMERCIAL VEHICLES
SHIPS
MANNED SPACEFLIGHT

The Arts etc
ARCHITECTURE
CATHEDRALS
CHURCHES
HERALDRY
FLAGS
PAINTING
MODERN ART
SCULPTURE
FURNITURE
MUSIC
POSTAGE STAMPS
POTTERY AND PORCELAIN

Sport
ASSOCIATION FOOTBALL
CRICKET

Cities
LONDON

The Observer's Book of
SHIPS

FRANK E. DODMAN

WITH 8 COLOUR PLATES
BLACK AND WHITE PHOTOGRAPHS
AND NUMEROUS LINE DRAWINGS

FREDERICK WARNE & CO LTD
FREDERICK WARNE & CO INC
LONDON : NEW YORK

ACKNOWLEDGEMENT

All the line drawings and unacknowledged photographs are
by the author.

LIBRARY OF CONGRESS CATALOG
CARD NO 73-80246

ISBN 0 7232 1517 0

Printed in Great Britain by
William Clowes & Sons, Limited
London, Beccles and Colchester
538.673

CONTENTS

LIST OF COLOUR PLATES

PREFACE

The main purpose of this book is to introduce the observer to the wide variety of ships that he may see within the four main categories: merchant ships, warships, fishing vessels and sail school-ships, and to provide him with some general background information about ships and the sea. Previous editions have included a brief history of ships and a small section on the rigs of yachts and small boats. These have now been omitted so that the other sections could be extended. In this entirely new edition the line drawings, silhouettes and photographs have been distributed throughout the text in a way that should make the book easier to use 'in the field'.

Like other major transport organizations, both the administration and the working units of the shipping industry are constantly changing. New types of vessels appear as others lose their importance; the rapid world-wide development of the container system and the run-down of the passenger service liner are but two examples of such far-reaching changes. A larger selection of flags and funnels than in the previous edition is included in the colour section although here, too, it is not easy to keep abreast of the visual results of mergers and take-overs. The P & O fleet, for instance, now consists of twenty or so shipping companies and it will be several years before the funnels and hull colours are changed; some, in the Short Sea Division, may retain their present distinctive liveries.

The adoption of the metric system in the marine industry has, as far as this book is concerned, resulted in the following usage. Ship lengths, and other linear measurements are given in *metres* and gun calibres in *millimetres*. Any reference to weight, such as deadweight, lightweight or displacement is expressed in *tonnes*; for the purpose of the ordinary observer the difference between *tons* and *tonnes* is only slight. *Tonnes* is also used in connection with the maximum lifting power of cargo derricks. The register *ton* of 100 ft³, as in *gross tons*, remains as an international measurement of capacity. The *nautical mile* and the *knot* continue to be used as international units only and are fractionally different from the UK units. Brake horse-power, used here with reference to tugs, will eventually be expressed in kW units.

In a book of this type information is compiled from diverse sources. Special acknowledgement is however due to that invaluable source, *Jane's Fighting Ships*, edited by R. V. B. Blackman. Thanks are due to the Meteorological Office, and to the Controller, HM Stationery Office, for his permission to reproduce flags, and a selection of signals, from the International Code of Signals which was revised in April 1969. The Ministry of Defence (Navy) and the Naval Attachés in London of the United States, France, Italy and Sweden generously lent photographs for reproduction and acknowledgement is made in the relevant places. Thanks are also due to the many shipping companies who provided information on their liveries and services, and gave technical details of their ships. Where they also lent photographs for reproduction, their assistance is recognized in the captions. Some of the author's photographs were taken with the permission of dock authorities and, therefore, thanks are due to the Manchester Ship Canal Company, the Mersey Docks and Harbour Company, and the Forth Ports Authority.

Fig. 1 Cunard passenger and cruise liner *Queen Elizabeth 2*

Fig. 2 The P & O Passenger Division's new 17,000-ton cruise liner, *Spirit of London*. She is based on the West Coast of USA

1 GENERAL INFORMATION Part I
INTRODUCTION

The observer's powers of observation, and his knowledge of ships, generally pass through the following stages:

(*a*) Recognition of the main *groups:* merchant ships, warships, fishing vessels, pleasure craft, sailing vessels, harbour craft.

(*b*) Recognition of the main *types* within these groups, so that he knows the difference between a passenger liner and a cargo liner, a cruiser and a destroyer, a trawler and a drifter.

(*c*) Recognition of the *varieties* within each type —the difference between a fruit carrier and a fast cargo liner, a guided missile destroyer and an anti-submarine destroyer, a barquentine and a topsail schooner.

With his expanding knowledge of types he acquires skill in estimating the *tonnage*, *length* and *speed* of most ships that he sees. At a later stage, by the hull form, funnel shape, character of super-structure and ventilator, davit or crane, he can guess at the approximate *date of building*.

He begins to know the *company character* of many merchant ships and immediately recognizes a Blue Funnel or a Clan liner by design alone. An experienced observer knows many *individual* ships and can state their owners, nationality, tonnage, speed, service and many other details of interest. At the same time he gradually develops his knowledge of flags.

In a pocket book of this size there is no space for merchant, naval and fishing fleet lists, but the illustrations and notes provide information on many aspects of ships which will be of service to the observer who pursues his interest in the docks, along the shore, at sea—or even from the air.

9

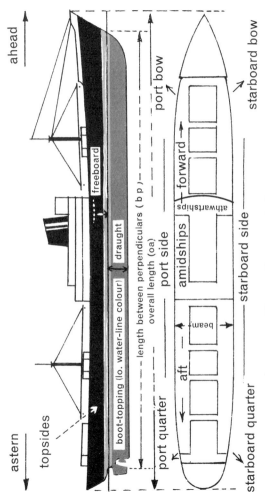

Fig. 3 Some nautical terms

Nautical Terms

Abaft Towards the ship's stern. **Abeam** In a line at right angles to the ship's length. Abreast. **Aft** Towards the ship's stern. **Ahead** In advance of the ship's bows. **Amidships** Near the centre of the ship's length. **Astern** Behind the ship. **Athwartships** From one side of the ship to another. **Athwart** Transversely. **Awash** Level with the surface of the water. **Aweigh** Anchor just raised from the sea-bed. **Beam** Greatest breadth of the ship. **Bows** Foremost part of a ship. **Cable** or **cable-length** One tenth of a nautical mile, 185·2 m (600 ft) or 100 fathoms. **Camber** Athwartship upward curve of a ship's deck. **Fathom** One hundredth part of a cable (1·82 m or 6 ft). **Flare** or **Flam** The outward and upward curve of a ship's side at the bows. **Forward** Towards the bows. **Knot** Unit of speed. A nautical mile traversed in one hour. **Leeward** Direction to which the wind is blowing. **Lee** Sheltered side away from the wind. **Nautical Mile** One minute of latitude at the equator. Mean nautical mile = 1,852 m. Ten cables. **Port** Left-hand side when looking towards the bows. Earlier known as **larboard.** **Quarter** Direction between *abeam* and *astern* and that part of a vessel's sides near the stern. **Rake** Slope of a funnel, masts or stem. **Sheer** Fore-and-aft curve of a hull or deck, rising towards bows and stern. **Starboard** Right-hand side when looking towards the bows. **Trim** Way a vessel sits in the water, i.e. on an even keel, down by the head, or down by the stern. **Tumblehome** Upward and inward curve of a vessel's side. **Wake** Foamy water left in track of a ship. **Way** and **Under way** Passage of a ship through the water. **Windward** Direction from which the wind is blowing.

Tonnage

Ship tonnage sometimes confuses the layman, particularly when he finds that one ship can have five different figures, the highest often three times larger than the lowest. Any comparison between tonnage figures must obviously refer to the same sort of tonnage for each of the ships concerned. It is important to distinguish between the two terms *tons* and *tonnes*; the former refers to cubic capacity and the latter to weight in metric tonnes. With regard to merchant ships, *gross*, *net* and *deadweight* tonnage figures are normally used. There is no hard-and-fast relationship between these figures and, unless the ships are of the same type with the same functions, comparisons are apt to be misleading. Tonnage measured by capacity is based on the international unit of 100 ft^3, or 2·83 m^3 equal to one ton. The latter term does not, therefore, refer to weight as it is derived from the earlier *tun*, which indicated the capacity of a wine cask.

Gross registered tonnage (g.r.t. or gt) is the total of all permanently enclosed space above and below decks, with certain exceptions such as the wheelhouse, chart room, radio room, galley, washing facilities and other specified spaces above deck.

Net registered tons (n.r.t.) is the earning space of the ship, i.e. the gross tonnage less the crew's accommodation, steering gear and anchor working space, workshops, ballast tanks and the space for the propelling machinery. Port and harbour dues are calculated on net tonnage. Certain ships are classified as open/closed shelter deck vessels (see page 30). The triangular tonnage mark indicates that certain modified or alternative tonnages have been assigned to the ship.

Fig. 4

Plimsoll or
International
Convention
Loadlines and
Tonnage Mark

Tonnage by weight
is the weight
of water displaced
by the vessel. **Light
displacement** is

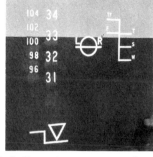

the weight of the ship's hull, engines, spares and
other items necessary for her working. **Load
displacement** is the ship's weight when fully
laden, i.e. hull, engines, cargo, crew and every-
thing on board sinking her down to the summer
draught loadline. **Deadweight** (d.w. or dwt) is
the difference between *light* and *load* displacement
and therefore gives the weight—in metric tonnes—
of the cargo, ballast, fresh water, fuel, crew and
passengers.

Displacement tonnages are calculated in relation
to draught and the statutory freeboard which must
be shown on the ship's side along with the above
markings (**Fig. 4**). Above the latter is a short
horizontal line giving the level of the vessel's deck
line; the difference between that and the line
through the circle is the freeboard. On the grid
the letters signify: LR Lloyd's Register (the
assigning authority), TF Tropical Fresh Water,
F Fresh Water, T Tropical Salt Water, S Summer
Salt Water, W Winter Salt Water and WNA
Winter North Atlantic. These loading marks allow
for the different specific gravities; with the same
cargo, a ship will sink deeper into the water in
seas near the equator than she will in the North
Atlantic, in winter.

Methods of Mechanical Propulsion

Steam reciprocating engines The first passenger steamship was the *Comet* of 1812, propelled by a simple 4–h.p. engine driving at first two pairs of paddles, and later one. Fuel consumption was large and consequently her trips were short; all early steamships suffered from the handicap of excessive fuel consumption. The simple engine developed into the two-cylinder compound engine and eventually became the triple-expansion compound engine. The latter was slow, but economical and reliable, and although it was the only method of driving paddles and propellers for nearly a hundred years, it is used now only in a few large trawlers, some tugs and the older dredgers, and in a few surviving wartime merchant ships. Steam is generated in Scotch fire-tube boilers, passes through a small high-pressure cylinder, a medium-pressure and then, the largest, low-pressure cylinder.

Steam reaction turbines Acting on a principle similar to that of the water-wheel, the steam—generated in water-tube boilers—passes through numerous fine nozzles onto small blades fixed round the rim of a cylinder, thus forcing it to revolve. The average turbine revolves at a speed of about 4,000 r.p.m. and before this power can be transmitted to the propeller shaft the rotational speed must be reduced through single, or double, reduction gearing down to about 100 r.p.m. This mechanically simple type of engine is efficient, quiet and smooth running, and is used today in many passenger liners, fast cargo liners, and container ships, many tankers, some cross-Channel ferries and the majority of warships.

Electric propulsion is used when the shafts are connected to electric motors for which the current is provided by either steam turbo- or diesel-driven generators. This method is not very common, used only by some tankers built in the 1940s, a very few liners—the *Canberra* is a modern one—and some diesel-electric trawlers and dredgers.

Diesel motors   The general principle of the marine engine is similar to that of the motor-car internal combustion engine except that the oil fuel is ignited by compression.   Compared with the steam engine the fuel consumption is low, and the fact that no fuel is consumed at all when the ship is in port is an advantage.   This type of engine is now common for almost every type of merchant ship.

Gas turbines   Free piston gas turbines were introduced in the late 1950s after a number of experiments in ocean-going ships.   The principle is similar to that of the steam turbine but the hot gas provides the motive force to the blades— direct rotary action.   In some power installations part of the power is provided by diesel engines, and the gas exhaust from these operates a gas turbine to give additional power.   The system is very reliable, easy to maintain and takes up much less space than other methods of propulsion.   Some warships are now propelled by this method, while others have combined systems such as COSOG— steam and gas or CODOG—diesel engines and gas turbine according to the type of ship.

Nuclear reactors   In this new type of marine propulsion a nuclear heat-productivity unit provides steam for conventional low-pressure turbines.   The most important advantage is that, using a very small amount of fuel, the vessel can remain at sea for many months without refuelling. This is of great value to the warship, and in particular to the submarine, and the system has therefore first come into general use in submarines.

Fig. 5
Kort
nozzle

The United States Navy does however possess
nuclear-powered ships in nearly every important
category. Nuclear power units are extremely
expensive and, as a result, very few merchant
ships have been operated with this form of propulsion. The cargo-passenger liner *Savannah*,
built in 1959, was the first with a pressurized water
reactor and compound double-reduction geared
turbines. She was not intended to be economical,
but served as an ocean-going experimental laboratory for the marine reactor while carrying cargo
and passengers. The German cargo liner *Otto
Hahn*, the Russian icebreaker *Lenin* and the
Japanese *Mutsu* are nuclear-powered vessels.

Changes in methods of propulsion have not been
confined to power units; other developments have
contributed to greater manoeuvrability and more
economical use of fuel. In the **Kort nozzle**
(**Fig. 5**) unit the propeller, shrouded by a short
open-ended cylinder, increases pushing power by
about 25 per cent, with a consequent saving in fuel
costs. If vanes of aerofoil section are fitted, the
normal rudder can be dispensed with. This unit
reduces vibration and gives better control so that a
vessel can turn in a very tight circle; it is mainly
used by fishing vessels and tugs.

The **controllable pitch propeller** has 3 or 4 blades, each one of which can turn on its own axis to give greater efficiency under varying conditions and has the advantage that, when going astern, the rotation of the propeller shaft is not reversed.

Many ships of all types and sizes are now equipped with a **bow thruster unit** in which a reversible propeller is situated in a transverse tunnel passing through the hull near the bows. This propeller forces water to one side or the other, as required, and greatly assists movements in docks.

The **Voith-Schneider** cycloidal propeller works rather like a feathered paddle-wheel placed on a vertical instead of a horizontal axis in the bottom of the vessel's hull. Spade-shaped blades project from near the edge of a disc which rotates on a vertical axis; by changing the relative angle of the blades the thrust can be exerted in any direction without the use of a rudder. This type of unit is particularly successful in shallow and confined waters.

The **bulbous bow** reduces pitching, and for tankers and freighters it increases speed when they are sailing in ballast. **Stabilizers** are projecting fins, fitted to passenger ships below the water-line, to reduce the effect of rolling in rough weather.

Fig. 6
Bulbous
bow

Basic Hull Forms Stems and Sterns

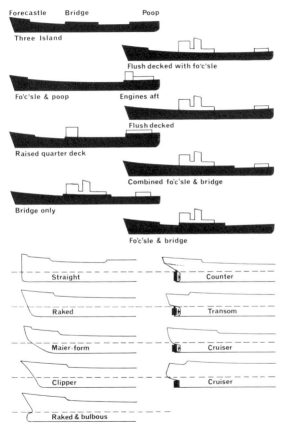

Fig. 7 Basic hull forms, stems and sterns

18

2 MERCHANT SHIPS

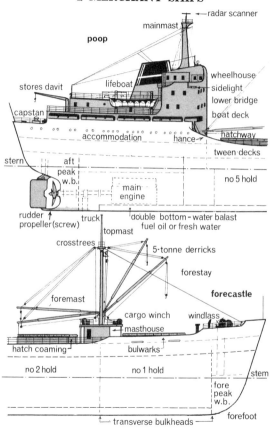

Fig. 8 Parts of a merchant ship

Fig. 9 Comparative silhouettes of ocean-going merchant ships

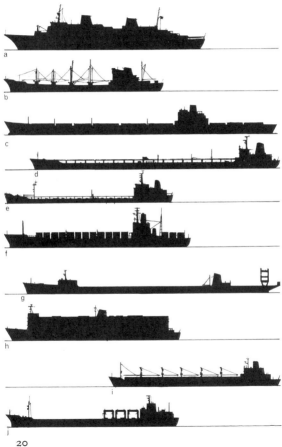

a Swedish **passenger liner** with accommodation for 750 passengers on North Atlantic service or 450 on cruises.* 1966/26,680 gt/210·20 m/M(2)/22 k

b Dutch general and refrigerated **cargo liner** on service between Europe and Gulf ports. 1963/7,200 gt/162 m/M/17 k

c World's first triple screw **container ship** on service Japan to Europe via Panama Canal. 1972/53,500 gt/269 m/M/31 k 1842 containers—deck cargo not shown.

d British **crude oil tanker** 1965/67,579 dwt/248 m/M/15·5 k

e British **products tanker** 1968/15,922 dwt/169·40 m/M/14 k

f Japanese **container ship** for service between Japan and Pacific coast of North America—nearly 500 containers below deck and 212 above deck. 1969/16,500 gt/186 m/22–26 k

g Dutch/German **LASH** vessel carries 83 loaded barges between USA and Europe. 1972/43,000 dwt/261·40 m/M/18 k

h Norwegian **car carrier** converted from British passenger liner in 1971/18,000 gt/176·80 m/M(2)/18 k

i Swedish **bulk lumber carrier** with deck cargo. British Columbia to Europe. 1970/26,420 dwt/175·20 m/M/15·5 k

j Canadian **bulk forest products carrier** British Columbia to UK, part-return cargo of phosphate rock from Florida to British Columbia. Equipped with three travelling Monck loaders. 1969/21,461 gt/181 m/M/14·5 k

* Building date/tonnage/overall length/method of propulsion and number of screws if more than one/service speed.

Passenger/cruise liner

As the name suggests, this type of ship is designed to carry a large number of passengers. Sizes and silhouettes do vary considerably, and with the recent trend in 'individual' funnels many ships can be identified quite easily by this feature alone.

Fig. 10   MV* *Vistafjord* No/1973/24,000 gt/ 190·82 m/M(2)20 k/830 passengers

The profile of a passenger liner cannot be mistaken for any other type of ship. She has a high superstructure—often of four or more continuous decks—which occupies about three-quarters of the ship's overall length. On each side is a row of five or six lifeboats and many rectangular windows and, below this, the hull is pierced by long rows of cabin portholes on main, A, B, C and D decks. Forward of the navigating bridge, and aft of the superstructure, are pairs of derricks, or deck cranes, required for handling stores and possibly a very small amount of cargo. Quite a number of liners now have machinery aft and, like the *Canberra*, *Rotterdam* and *Hanseatic*, slender twin funnels. Only two of the giant transatlantic passenger liners now remain—the *Queen Elizabeth 2* and the *France*—and, owing to the decline in the Atlantic passenger trade, these ships are engaged in cruising during the winter months.

On other routes, too, passenger traffic is declining and many liners have been sold or con-

* In the captions MV stands for motor vessel.

verted for cruising. New ships are now being built solely for cruising. From the observer's point of view there is no difference between the passenger liner on regular service and the cruising liner. Some of the custom-built cruise liners of the seventies, such as the *Cunard Adventurer* and the *Song of Norway*, have deep clipper bows and a yacht-like appearance with emphasis on individual and often bizarre features such as the latter ship's funnel observation lounge. The drawing in **Fig. 10** illustrates a new liner with a traditional and very well-proportioned profile.

Fig. 11 SS *France* Fr/1961/66,348 gt/315·46 m/ ST(4)30 k

Fig. 12 TES *Canberra* Br/1961/44,807 gt/ 249·58 m/TE(2)/27·5 k

By courtesy of P & O

Fig. 13 Comparative profiles of passenger/cruise liners (1)

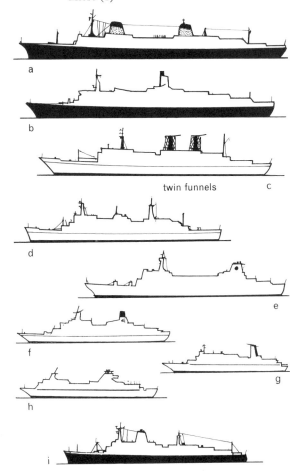

a

b

c

twin funnels

d

e

f

g

h

i

a *France* Fr/1961/66,348 gt/315·46 m/ST(4)/30 k/ 2,000 p.* The longest passenger ship in the world, this quadruple-screw liner is engaged on the North Atlantic Service and in cruising.

b *Queen Elizabeth 2* Br/1969/65,863 gt/293·51 m/ ST(2)28·5 k/2,025 p. A much smaller ship than the other two previous Cunard *Queens*, she is designed to pass through the Panama Canal. North Atlantic service and cruising.

c *Raffaello* It/1965/45,900 gt/275·80 m/ST(2)/ 27 k/1,775 p. This liner, and her sister *Michelangelo* are easily distinguished by the lattice structure surrounding the funnels.

d *Rotterdam* Ne/1959/37,783 gt/228·33 m/ST(2)/ 22 k/1,456 p. Transatlantic service and annual world cruise.

e *Oceanic* Pa/1965/27,645 gt/238·39 m/ST(2)/ 26 k/1,600 p. Designed for all-the-year-round cruising.

f *Royal Viking Star* No/1971/21,500 gt/177·10 m/ M(2)21·25 k/541 p. Owned jointly by three shipowners—one of three ships designed for world cruising.

g *Cunard Adventurer* Br/1971/14,155 gt/147·52 m/M(2)21·25 k/806 p. One-class liner for short range cruises in semi-tropical waters.

h *Song of Norway* No/1969/18,416 gt/168·3 m/ M(2)121 k/870 p. One of three sister ships designed for Caribbean luxury cruising. Deep clipper bow as **g**, can be distinguished by observation lounge built on unusual funnel structure.

i *Regina Magna* Gre/1938/32,360 gt/212·30 m /ST(4)/23 k/1,000 p. Originally French *Pasteur*, she later became the German *Bremen*—now one-class cruising liner.

* p refers to approximate number of passengers.

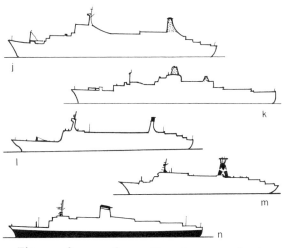

Fig. 14 Comparative profiles of passenger/cruise liners (2)

j *Canberra* Br/1961/44,807 gt/249·58 m/TE(2)/ 27·5 k/2,250 p.   UK to Australasia and cruising. Engines aft and slender twin funnels.

k *Oriana* Br/1960/41,910 gt/245·10 m/ST(2)/27·5 k /2,184 p.   Similar basic specifications to **j**, but different methods of propulsion, engines amidships and very different profile.

l *Eugenio C* It/1966/30,567 gt/217·30 m/ST(2)/ 27 k/1,600 p.   With twin funnels aft, this liner bears some resemblance to *Canberra* and *Rotterdam*. South Atlantic service and cruising.

m *Hamburg* Ge/1968/25,000 gt/195·00 m/ST(2)/ 23 k/790 p.   On Atlantic service and cruising. Twelve decks.   Funnel unlike any other liner.

n *Leonardo da Vinci* It/1960/33,340 gt/233·80 m/ ST(2)25·5 k/1,326 p.   Atlantic service.

26

Fig. 15 MV *Centaur*
Br/1964/7,990
gt/146·40 m
/M(2)/20 k

Passenger/cargo liner

The terms passenger/cargo and cargo/passenger are self-explanatory and distinguish the class from ships designed as single-purpose carriers. In the last twenty years the number of dual-purpose liners has been drastically reduced, and it looks as though this type will soon become obsolete. Shipowners find that not only is there a considerable drop in the need for berths, but the combination of passenger and cargo carrying is not economic. In appearance the type is a smaller version of the normal passenger liner, but has a smaller superstructure, fewer boats, and obvious cargo-handling gear.

The drawing shows such a vessel built for the Blue Funnel Line and designed to carry 200 passengers on her run between Western Australia and Malaysia. In addition to general, refrigerated and liquid cargo, she has accommodation for 4,500 sheep, 40 dairy cattle and 700 other cattle. This unusual cargo is to provide Moslems with livestock which they can slaughter in accordance with their religious customs. Many of the surviving passenger/cargo liners previously on the North and South Atlantic now operate in Eastern waters, where there is still some need for them.

Fig. 16 MV *Monte Umbe* Sp/1959/
9,971 gt/154·83 m/16.5 k/300 p

*By courtesy of
Aznar Line*

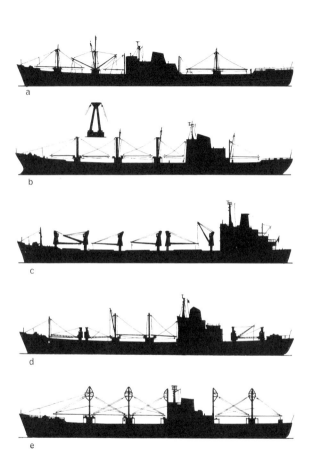

Fig. 17 Variations of the cargo liner

Cargo liner

The ocean-going dry cargo liner, with a gross tonnage of between 5,000 and 12,000 gross tons, is designed for the transport of cargoes of many different types, shapes and sizes. The term *liner* is given to a vessel which operates on a regular service between ports, whereas the term *tramp* is given to a ship employed on charter to take cargo from port to port at any time, anywhere in the world. The cargo liner—referred to as a *freighter* in some countries—has four or five holds, and one or two tween decks which run for practically the full length of the ship, so that the varied items of cargo can be methodically stowed for convenient access at the relevant ports of discharge, and the weight of the cargo can more

---

a *Lobito Palm* Br/1960/5,923 gt/144·41 m/M/16 k. Machinery amidships and five holds served by sixteen single derricks and a heavy lift jumbo derrick.

b *Benefactor* Br/1971/11,299 gt/164·21 m/M/18 k. Engines three-quarter aft with holds served by sixteen derricks and three jumbos. Bipod masts and single kingposts. Bulbous bow (Fig. 6).

c *Birkaland* Sw/1969/9,640 gt/139·94 m/M/16·5 k. Machinery aft and six deck cranes.

d *Majestic* Br/1967/12,277 gt/164·6 m/M/19 k. Mixture of derricks and cranes.

e *Taupo* Br/1966/8,219 gt/160·93 m/M/20 k. Fast general and refrigerated cargo liner distinguished by patent Hallen 30-tonne derricks which are developed from the simple derrick so that all slewing and topping actions can be operated by one man at each derrick.

easily be distributed. Until recently the cargo liner usually had machinery amidships, with an even placing of the holds fore and aft, but the recent trend is for the propelling machinery, and bridge superstructure to be either right aft or three-quarter aft.

Increased cargo space is made available in the shelter deck type of vessel. In the *closed shelter deck* (CSD) vessel, the transverse bulkheads are carried right up to the shelter deck; in the *open shelter deck* (OSD) they are carried only as far as the main deck. In the latter type a small $1 \cdot 21$–m square opening is cut in the shelter deck and arranged so that it cannot be permanently closed.* Recent changes in tonnage assessment mean that a shelter deck vessel may have an alternative tonnage mark painted on the hull (see page 13) so that the registered tonnage is assessed—open or closed—according to which tonnage mark is submerged.

The cargo-handling gear is obviously an important distinguishing feature of the cargo liner. It is arranged so as to ensure the minimum delay in loading or discharging cargo from all the holds and, if necessary, over both sides of the ship at the same time. Many ships now have deck cranes, or a mixture of cranes and derricks, patent Stülcken (page 32) or Hallen derricks or Monck loaders (**Fig. 9j**). The simple mast, stayed by wire shrouds, is fast disappearing as strongly built self-supporting single and bipod masts take its place, with considerable reduction in maintenance costs and less obstruction during working operations.

---

* Under these conditions the space between the main and shelter decks is not included in the registered tonnage on which harbour dues are calculated.

Fig. 18 MV *Novelist*
Br/1965/5,580 gt/124·05 m/16 k

A three-quarter aft cargo liner equipped with derricks, deck cranes and, right aft, a swinging-type Stülcken derrick, she has a short fore-castle and the bridge superstructure is at the forward end of a long poop.   The vessel is in a light condition, i.e. with little or no cargo aboard.

Fig. 19

250-tonne Stulcken derricks

MV *Craftsman*
Br/1972/
10,500 gt/
162·15 m/
M/18·5 k

Heavy lift cargo liner

For many years a Norwegian shipping company
specialized in transporting heavy loads such as
railway locomotives, rolling-stock, barges and tugs.
In recent years a number of other companies have
equipped some of their vessels with German
patent Stülcken derricks capable of lifting loads of
up to 180 tonnes. This new type of derrick is
quite distinctive in appearance; from the beam
view the unstayed derrick posts are much heavier
than the usual type, and from any other viewpoint
their marked upward splay can easily be seen.
The derricks are much easier to operate than the
conventional heavy-lift derrick and they can work
either longitudinally, serving hatches fore or aft
or outboard over the quayside. When working
in the latter position the ship's potential list is
counteracted by water ballast heeling tanks.

The silhouette shows a Harrison ship fitted with
two Stülcken derricks together capable of lifting
loads up to about 500 metric tonnes. The vessel is
also equipped with normal deck cranes, 10-tonne
derricks and a Stülcken new type of swinging
derrick to serve the aftermost hold and handle
general cargo.

Fig. 20 MV *Custodian* Br/1961/8,847 gt/149·05
m/16 k with 110-tonne Stülcken heavy lift gear

Fig. 21 MV *Booker Vanguard*
Br/1963/5,417 gt/122·81 m/15·5 k

This cargo liner is designed for the transport of
general cargo between the UK and Central
America, returning from the West Indies with a
bulk cargo of sugar, greenheart logs and rum.
She is seen here in a fully loaded condition, before
discharge of her cargo. The cargo-handling
equipment consists of Stülcken swinging derricks
and deck cranes.

Fig. 22 MV *Papendrecht*
Ne/1961/8,947 gt/152·40 m/15 k

A flush-decked and raised forecastle type of
cargo liner with engines amidships and a cruiser
stern. Her cargo-handling equipment consists of
sixteen single derricks and a heavier lift jumbo
derrick at the foremast.

33

Fig. 23 SS *Benalder* Br/1972/49,700 dwt/
288·33 m/ST(2)/27 k (2,687 6·09 m containers)

Container ship

During recent years an important development
has taken place in the handling and transport of
rail, road and seaborne freight with the introduction of the container, or unit/system. Traditional systems have involved numerous crates of
miscellaneous shapes and sizes handled by different types of ships or quayside cranes. A
completely integrated system has now emerged
based on the use of standard ISO (International
Standards Organization) box units of agreed
dimensions: 2·43 m high and wide, and either
3·04, 6·09, 9·14 or 12·19 metres in length. The
majority of containers are designed for general dry
cargo, but specialized units can take liquid, powder
or refrigerated cargoes. Specially designed road
vehicles, railway wagons, ships and dockside equipment handle these units in a co-ordinated way with
speed and efficiency, and a minimum of manpower,
providing a door-to-door service.

The container ship has a high freeboard and the
superstructure is either right aft, or as in the
drawing, three-quarter aft. The deck, with
neither sheer nor camber, is unobstructed so that
containers can be stacked on it in addition to those
stowed below in the cellular holds. Handling of
containers is by dockside transporter cranes and
truck lifts, so that the vessel herself has only one or
two small derricks for handling stores. Some of
the container ships have stern or side doors so that
road vehicles can drive aboard with their container
loads.

Ocean-going container ships are very expensive to build; therefore the general policy is for them to be owned, and operated, by a consortium of shipping companies (sometimes of different nationalities) with common interests on a particular route. For instance the Atlantic Container Line is formed of French, British, Dutch, German and Swedish interests, and Overseas Containers Ltd is composed of several British companies running a weekly service from the UK to Australia.

Fig. 24 MV *Manchester Concorde* Br/1969/12,040 gt/161·50 m/19·5 k. On service between Manchester and Montreal lying at 25-tonne transporter cranes

Fig. 25 SS *Encounter Bay* Br/1969/ 26,756 gt/227·42 m/ST/21·5 k (OCL)

courtesy of P & O

Refrigerated ship or reefer

The refrigerated fruit carrier is a medium-sized but fast cargo liner capable of speeds up to 22 knots. Usually painted white, she has no particular characteristics to distinguish her from the general cargo liner, although some vessels do have a long forecastle or a combined bridgedeck and forecastle. The reefer is generally a very elegant looking vessel. The fruit is carried in compartments insulated with cork, glass wool or other

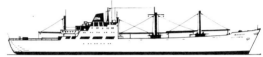

Fig. 26 MV *Persimmoncore* Is/1968/OSD/CSD 5,927/8,185 gt/147·80 m/19·5 k

material, and kept at a temperature between − 30° C and 12° C, according to the requirements of the fruit, each type needing a different temperature to keep it in good condition during the voyage.

Reefers in the fast fruit trade between South Africa and Europe are equipped to carry a wide range of fruits such as citrus fruits and deciduous apples and pears, whereas the ships on the West Indies to Europe trade usually specialize in carrying bananas. The *Geestport**** (**Fig. 27**) is owned by a combined British and Dutch company, carrying bananas to the ripening and distribution centres at Barry and Preston. Other well-known companies with reefers are Lauritzen (Denmark), Sven Salen (Sweden) and Fyffes of Britain.

The refrigerated meat carrier similarly has no

---

* Now the Greek *Kimolos* with a Norwegian sister ship.

particular outward feature for identification. Larger than the fruit carrier, she sails over much longer distances such as the Australia, New Zealand/UK and River Plate/UK runs. The chilled and frozen cargoes are carried in insulated holds at temperatures much lower than that required for fruit; these larger ships also carry general cargo. Companies associated with this type of cargo are the Blue Star Line, operating meat and general cargo services between South America, South Africa, New Zealand, Australia and the UK, and between Australia, New Zealand and the east coast of North America, and also the P & O general cargo division. The latter company has a series of 10,000–tonne dwt reefers for the carriage of fruit and refrigerated goods.

By courtesy of Geest Line

Fig. 27   Banana carrier MV *Geestport*
Br/1964/7,891 gt/148·73 m/21 k

Specially designed refrigerated ship which can carry 200,000 stems of bananas from the Windward Islands and Barbados to the UK, and British manufactured goods on the outward voyage. She has accommodation for twelve passengers.

Short-sea trader

Generally well under 3,000 gross tons, the short-sea trader operates in the North Sea, Baltic, English Channel, Mediterranean, or in similar waters in any part of the world. She often runs, like the ocean-going liner, to a fixed schedule

Fig. 28 MV *Silvio*
Br/1968/1,523
gt/93·80 m/13 k

between ports. Modern vessels have machinery aft and a short, stocky superstructure similar to the contemporary cargo liner. The short-sea trader may carry any type of cargo whether it is pre-palletised, unit load, container or in the conventional mixed form. Well-equipped with cargo-handling gear, the ship is able to load or discharge in small ports where facilities may be limited.

The silhouette shows a good example of the modern short-sea cargo liner built to carry goods in many forms between the UK and Scandinavia, or the Mediterranean. Additional features are

Fig. 29 MV *Mediterranian*
Br/1968/1,460 gt/94·14 m/13 k

Fig. 30   MV *Moss Maroc* Da/1971/
499 gt/75·20 m/12 k

the wide hatches and side loading doors which
give greater cargo-handling flexibility. High
capacity lifting-gear consists of two 25-tonne
Thomson derricks, two 5-tonne deck cranes and
two fork lifts. The holds and tween decks are
mechanically ventilated for the carriage of
Mediterranean citrus fruits. An increasing number of short-sea traders are now built to carry standard containers; in appearance these ships
resemble their larger ocean-going counterparts.

The photograph opposite shows a ship almost
identical with the silhouette and owned by the
same parent company. The main difference in
appearance is in the cargo gear, as this ship has no
deck cranes, and its derricks have a maximum
lifting capacity of 10 tonnes. The illustration
shows the transom, or economy stern referred to
on page 18. An unusual feature is the narrow
four-deck superstructure which incorporates a
goal-post for the No 2 hold derricks. The
permanent plastic awning over the whole of the
after deck indicates that the ship operates in a hot
zone for at least part of her time. **Fig. 30** shows a
Danish ship, with a bulbous bow, which is
similar to the *Mediterranian* in many features.

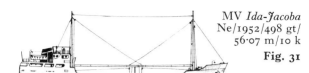

MV *Ida-Jacoba*
Ne/1952/498 gt/
56·07 m/10 k

Fig. 31

Coaster

No hard and fast rule can be drawn between the coaster and the short-sea trader. No particular vessel can, therefore, be identified primarily as a coaster, as the small freighter between 300 and 1,500 gross tons may be on charter (tramping), coasting or carrying cargo on short-sea scheduled service. Many well-known British coastal shipping companies have now ceased to exist owing to the development of heavy road transport. Much of the remaining traffic is confined to bulk cargoes of oil, coal, grain and fertilizers.

Many coasters with engines aft also have a raised quarter deck (page 18) which gives better trim when the ship is fully loaded. Another characteristic of the coaster, shared with the short-sea cargo and passenger ships, is the rubbing strake on each side of the hull just above the water-line.

Fig. 32 Estuarine motor barge

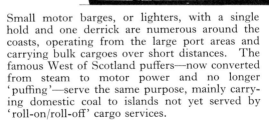

Small motor barges, or lighters, with a single hold and one derrick are numerous around the coasts, operating from the large port areas and carrying bulk cargoes over short distances. The famous West of Scotland puffers—now converted from steam to motor power and no longer 'puffing'—serve the same purpose, mainly carrying domestic coal to islands not yet served by 'roll-on/roll-off' cargo services.

The so-called 'Dutch' coaster sailing under the flags of the Netherlands, Germany, Denmark, Norway and France has now become a very familiar sight in almost every British and Continental port. The strongly-built hull allows the vessel to lie on the ground at low tide, and the squat funnel and superstructure, and hinged mast, set in a tabernacle, enables her to negotiate low bridges. Most of these coasters have a gross tonnage of just under 500, because of certain regulations about the number of crew and watch-keeping duties; as a result of these regula-

Fig. 33 Puffer

tions they are often referred to as 'paragraph' ships. With an average speed of 10 knots, comparatively powerful electric cargo-handling gear, and the features outlined above, the Dutch coaster is a handy vessel for service to upriver ports which may lack good quayside lifting-gear. Some of the coasters have their masts, or derricks, placed against the forecastle and the bridge superstructure so that the well deck is clear for the stowage of a deck cargo of timber.

Fig. 34 Dutch coaster *Dina* Ne/1954/298 gt/ 42·97 m/8·5 k discharging bags of fertilizer at the small upriver port of Perth

Oil Tanker (VLCC)

The first British tanker to exceed 100,000 tonnes deadweight was the *British Admiral*, which entered service in 1965 during a period of rapid change and development in the transport of oil. The increasing demand for oil products, and other economic factors, led to the inception of the giant tanker to carry crude oil from the oilfields in Central America, or the Persian Gulf, to the centres of population such as north-west Europe. Much less costly to operate than a number of smaller vessels, the 300–metre tanker soon became a common feature of world shipping.

The VLCC (very large crude carrier) is easily distinguished by her immense size and very simple

bulbous bow

Fig. 35 SS *British Explorer* Br/1970/215,603 dwt/325·80 m/ST/15·25 k

Fig. 36 SS *British Admiral* 1965/111,274 dwt/ 279·80 m/ST/16 k arriving at the BP terminal at Angle Bay, Pembrokeshire, with the motor tug *Thorngarth* in the foreground

Fig. 37
The same
VLCC with the mani-
fold connected up to
the shore installation.
Deck cranes replace
the normal hose-
handling derrick
By courtesy of BP

outline with a single bridge structure placed close
to the stern. Many of the ships have a bulbous bow,
but when the ship is down to her marks, it cannot
be seen.

The majority of crude oil tankers are single-
screw vessels propelled by steam turbines. With
her very deep draught, the giant tanker's activities are limited to a few terminal ports; two
methods of discharging the oil have been developed
to offset this disadvantage. One method is to
offload the cargo into smaller tankers in a deep,
but sheltered, anchorage somewhere near the
refineries, and the other is to discharge at a
deepwater terminal and pump the oil overland to
the refineries. Finnart, on Loch Long in the West
of Scotland, is a terminal of the latter kind.

By courtesy of BP

Fig. 38 SS *Spyros* Lib/1964/61,028 dwt/236·22
m/ST/16·5 k A fully-laden tanker off Spithead
on the way to the oil refineries at Fawley

43

Products tanker

The specialized carrier of oil in bulk now represents about one-third of the world total shipping tonnage. The products tanker is designed to transport either *clean* oil, i.e. motor spirit or kerosene, or *black* oil such as fuel and diesel oil, from refineries to discharge ports from whence it is distributed by road, rail, pipeline or sea. The giant crude oil tanker is a new development, but the conventional tanker has also increased in average size and is changing in appearance. In silhouette it retains the long, low outline, but the traditional three-island shape (**Fig. 40**) is giving way to the all-aft construction with the funnel, or twin funnels, bridge and accommodation all forming a single block on the poop (**Fig. 41**). In either form the islands are connected by a raised fore-and-aft gangway, or catwalk, which enables members of the crew to move from one island to another with safety in rough weather. This catwalk helps to identify the tanker and distinguish it from other bulk carriers. Additional characteristics are the numerous small tank hatches, many fore-and-aft running pipes and, amidships, the manifold with its complex arrangement of pipes

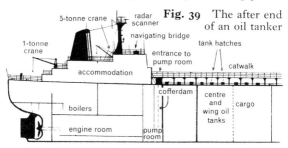

Fig. 39 The after end of an oil tanker

5-tonne crane

radar scanner

navigating bridge

1-tonne crane

entrance to pump room

tank hatches

catwalk

accommodation

cofferdam

centre and wing oil tanks

cargo

boilers

engine room

pump room

Fig. 40 MV *British Kestrel*
Br/1962/15,922 dwt/160·62 m/14·15 k

and valves connected to the ship's tank system.

The manifold is the focal point of the loading operations—by gravity or shore pumps—and discharging, by means of the ship's own pumps. Close to it are two light hose-handling derricks. The tanker hull is divided by two longitudinal and many transverse bulkheads forming up to thirty

Fig. 41 MV *British Liberty*
Br/1968/24,000 dwt/169·73 m/16 k

or so centre and wing cargo tanks. This number of comparatively small compartments minimizes the swishing effect of the liquid cargo and also means that several grades of oil can be carried on one voyage. At both ends of the cargo space there are double watertight bulkheads, known as cofferdams, in order to reduce the risk of fire spreading to the highly inflammable cargo. Smaller tankers are usually propelled by diesel engines and larger tankers by steam turbines, although this is not a general rule. In two of the largest tanker fleets, the BP group have almost equal numbers of motor and turbine vessels, whereas over 80 per cent of Shell tankers are propelled by steam turbines. As the tanker transports her cargo on only one way of a round voyage, her crew spend the 'in ballast' run cleaning the tanks and preparing for the next cargo.

Fig. 42

MV *Esso Ipswich*
Br/1961/1,570 dwt/
70·40 m/10 k

Coastal spirit tanker

The coastal spirit tanker is a smaller version of the
ocean-going tanker. Her trips are usually short
and she may be employed on the same route
between two ports for many months, or even years.
Obviously her loading port is one of the oil refineries where the spirit is produced; most ports
have storage tanks into which her cargo is discharged, preparatory to further distribution. The
coastal tanker has two islands—a short forecastle
and a poop with a single bridge superstructure—
which may be joined by a raised section of the hull
known as a trunk. The lower level deck on each
side of the trunk deck is only a few centimetres
above the water-line when the vessel is loaded.
As the tank tops are thoroughly watertight, this
very small freeboard presents no dangers.

Fig. 43

MV *Humbergate*
Br/1969/2,861 dwt/
84·64 m/12 k

A coastal tanker lying at a discharge berth with her
cargo pipe-line connected up to the shore installation. She has a low catwalk running between the
main superstructure and the forecastle.

LPG carrier

The liquefied gas carrier is distinguished from the normal oil tanker, or bulk carrier, by the elaborate deck fittings and pipe work, and the horizontal pressure cylinders. On some ships there is a series of large conical or domed tank tops visible above deck level. This type of vessel is specially

|— trunk deck and pressure tanks —————|

Fig. 44 MV *Roland* Sw/1968/
14,180 gt/166·12 m/16·5 k

designed for the carriage of: propane, butane and natural gas methane. Liquefied methane is carried in insulated tanks at a very low pressure and is cooled to its boiling-point. The mast amidships contains the vents from each tank. Like the oil tanker and bulk carrier, the ship has a number of wing and hopper tanks for water ballast.

Fig. 45 MV *Melrose* Br/1971/1,998 gt/86·95 m/
13·5 k. A fully/semi-refrigerated Ethylene/LPG tanker

By courtesy of Geo. Gibson & Co. Ltd

Bulk carrier

At first glance the bulk carrier may be mistaken for an oil tanker, as the long low silhouette and compact bridge superstructure are very similar, but on closer examination it will be seen that the bulk carrier lacks the catwalk and deck details of the tanker. The majority of bulk carriers have no derricks except a pair on the forecastle, or poop, for handling ship's stores. The loading and discharging of bulk cargoes—of grain, ore, cement, sugar, bauxite, industrial salt, phosphates or coal—is done by dockside cranes and grabs, and for this reason hatchways are wide and clear of obstructions. The silhouette line between the forecastle and the bridge may be broken by small projections

Fig. 46 MV *Laponia* Sw/1963/24,810 gt/ 202·72 m/15·5 k

which are either hold ventilators or part of the hatch control gear. The hatch covers are usually of the steel watertight patent type which are pulled clear of the hatches either by electric or hydraulic machinery. Some ore carriers do, however, have cargo-handling gear in order to permit the discharge of the cargo into barges alongside.

Many vessels are designed to carry alternative cargoes; some have the dual purpose of carrying large numbers of cars on the outward run and iron ore on the return voyage. Bulk carriers vary a good deal in size; one of the largest is the single-screw motor ship *Dunstanburgh Castle*, built in 1969, with a deadweight tonnage of over 100,000 tonnes.

Fig. 47 MV *Marianna* Ge/1962/14,782 gt/
172·50 m/14·5 k

A typical medium-sized bulk carrier with no
cargo-handling gear seen here discharging her
cargo of grain by means of dockside suction grain
elevators.

Fig. 48

MV *Sidney Bridge*
Br/1970/34,000 dwt/
224·02 m/15 k

The deck arrangement
of an ore carrier
showing the wide
hatches, with a
swimming-pool for the
crew between Nos 5
and 6. The short
mast forward has an
enclosed 'crow's nest'.

*By courtesy of
Bowring SS Co. Ltd*

oil hose derricks

hatches

Fig. 49 MV *Höegh Rainbow*
No/1970/101,193 dwt/
250·00 m/15·5 k

OBO carrier

The dual, or multi-purpose, bulk carrier has developed in order to eliminate the necessity of making long return voyages in ballast. The oil/bulk/ore ship's hull is subdivided so that the holds for the bulk cargo, such as grain or ore, are flanked by oil tanks. There are also oil tanks between the floors of the holds and the ship's bottom. The OBO can be distinguished from the normal bulk carrier by the more elaborate hybrid deck fittings, with oil tank vents and piping—and a manifold—as well as the wide steel hatch covers. At a distance the additional feature of the central hose derricks can be picked out. As the 100,000 tonne deadweight OBO s are very costly vessels they are, like so many of the container ships, owned by a consortium of companies such as British Seabridge Shipping, whose ships have the word *Bridge* in their names.

Fig. 50 OBO *Tokyo* Sw/1967/42,534 gt/250·8
m/M/16 k   *Skyfotos, Ashford, Kent*

Car carrier

Mention has already been made of the bulk/car dual-purpose ship. Early in 1971 a new silhouette appeared on the shipping scene with the introduction of the Norwegian car carrier *Höegh Traveller* and, subsequently, her sister ships. The unusually long and very high superstructure

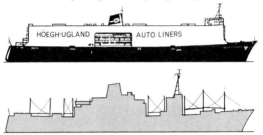

Fig. 51 MV *Höegh Traveller*
No/1960/18,575 gt/178·01 m/17·5 k

resembles the contemporary passenger-car ferry. The original ship was built in 1961—with two sister ships—as the Royal Mail Line's *Aragon*, a passenger and refrigerated cargo liner for the UK to South America service. The lower drawing shows her outline as she was at that time. In her present form, after extensive conversion, she now carries cars from Europe to America. In the 1960s some large freighters were built for the same purpose. The *Johann Schulte*, a 15,000-ton motor ship was designed as a dual-purpose vehicle bulk ship with holds equipped with hoistable false decks capable of holding 1,750 Volkswagen vehicles on the outward passage from Hamburg. On her return voyage, often through the St Lawrence Seaway, she carried either grain, or ore, in bulk.

LASH ship

In the early 1970s an entirely new conception of sea transport came into being with the introduction of the Lighter Aboard Ship (LASH) system. Vessels of this type are large, low ships with no sheer and very little superstructure. The navigation bridge is placed very far forward and the small twin athwartships funnels are towards the stern. A huge gantry crane, with a lifting capacity of about 500 tonnes, runs on 200-metre rails from close to the bridge to the stern. This crane is used to lift the laden lighters from water level (at the stern) to be stowed either in one of the five

Fig. 52 LASH ship MV *Bilderdyk*
Ne/1972/43,000 gt/261·40 m/18 k

holds or on deck. The ship can carry a total of 83 fully laden lighters—49 in the holds and 34 on deck. In port they are lifted from the stowed position, lowered to water level and towed away without the use of quay space.

The first LASH route was between New Orleans and Rotterdam and Sheerness—all three ports serving as centres of inland and intracoastal waterways linking large areas of industry and population. Other areas such as the Firth of Forth also serve as terminal anchorages for LASH services. The ship illustrated in **Fig. 52** is owned by the Holland–America and Hapag–Lloyd A.G. lines. The service provides a door-to-door transport method far into the interior of Europe or North America without need for quayside delays and handling.

Fig. 53
Aberthaw Fisher
Br/1966/2,355 gt/
83·52 m/
DE(2)/11 k

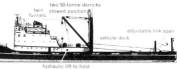

two 50-tonne derricks
stowed position

twin
funnels

adjustable link span

vehicle deck

hydraulic lift to hold

Heavy lift coaster

This unusual looking vessel is one of two specialized carriers built for James Fisher & Sons Ltd for the transport of very heavy, and difficult, items of machinery. For this purpose, one of them is on long-term charter to the Central Electricity Board for the transport of transformers and other bulky items required for the construction of power stations. The distinctive feature is the large central goal post with its two 50-tonne derricks which are stowed in the vertical position when the ship is at sea. The cargo, whether a transformer or a diesel locomotive, is winched across the link span at the stern on to the vehicle deck. At the forward end of this deck it is transferred to the hydraulic lift and then lowered into the hold. The link span at the stern can be raised or lowered to correspond with the level of the quay. As the superstructure is so far forward, and the long clear deck is an obvious feature, the heavy lift coaster may be mistaken for an oil rig supply vessel (page 69) or perhaps, at a distance, for a salvage tug.

Fig. 54 Looking forward along the vehicle deck of the *Aberthaw Fisher*

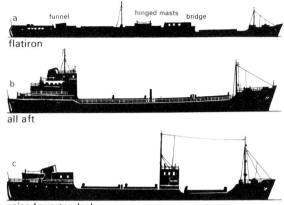

a   funnel   hinged masts   bridge

flatiron

b

all aft

c

raised quarter deck

Collier   **Fig. 55**   Three types of collier

The collier is a medium-sized bulk carrier which is normally operated on coastal and short-sea routes. Usually a single deck vessel, i.e. with no tween decks, it has three to five holds, very large hatches and high hatch coamings. No cranes or derricks are fitted, as the collier loads her cargo at gravity tips and discharges it at special wharves equipped with quayside grab cranes; the extra wide hatches give the grabs greater access to all parts of the holds. Sometimes the holds are U-shaped in section so that the cargo will tend to level out by gravity and trim itself; in this case the collier is referred to as 'self-trimming'.

Owing to the increase in the use of North Sea gas, and the development of oil-fired and nuclear power stations in Great Britain, the number of coastal colliers has been drastically reduced. Some of the Thames upriver colliers, known as *flatirons* (**Fig. 55**), so familiar to Londoners as they negotiated the bridges with lowered masts, have been sold and a few have gone into the grain trade. These *flatirons*, i.e. the motor ships, as all the steamships have gone, have a very low bridge, a hardly discernible funnel, and short masts which can be lowered on a hinged tabernacle. The middle drawing **b** shows a flush-decked collier with raised forecastle and machinery aft employed in carrying 7,000 tonnes of coal from the Humber and north-east ports to London and the south of England, at an average speed of twelve knots. The lower drawing **c** is a raised three-quarter deck motor collier, with an island bridge, employed in the UK and near-Continent trade, and in importing coal to Northern Ireland.

By courtesy of Cory Maritime Ltd

Fig. 56   MV *Corchester*
Br/1965/4,840 gt/112·80 m/12 k

A collier with the typical wide hatches and lack of derricks or deck cranes. This single deck ship, with four self-trimming holds, carries over 7,000 tonnes of small particle coal to power stations where it is discharged by quayside grabs.

RO/RO passenger/car ferry

The traditional cross-channel packet was a fast steam turbine vessel resembling a miniature passenger liner. With the widespread and continual growth of road transport, and the private car, this elegant type of ship has been almost entirely superseded by the much heavier-looking motor vessel with a high freeboard, three- or four-deck superstructure, and twin funnels placed athwartships. This latter arrangement allows unobstructed vehicle decks, although some of the ferries do retain the central funnel, and many of the twin funnel vessels even have a large central dummy funnel as well. These new ships are designed with facilities for quick loading and discharging so that car drivers themselves can drive on and off over hydraulically operated bow and/or stern ramps. In port the bow ramp, or vizor, can easily be recognized in its raised position, but at sea it forms an unobtrusive watertight closure.

Fig. 57 Deck arrangement of a ferry and MV *Prinz Hamlet II* Ge/1969/3,777 gt/103·03 m/22 k

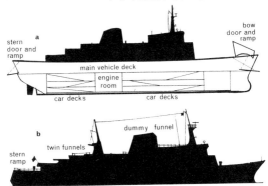

Fig. 58

Cars driving
through the
stern door of
a ferry on the
Newhaven/
Dieppe route

*By courtesy of
British Rail*

Not all the ferries have this bow ramp; some have
side doors instead, in addition to the universal
stern door and ramp.

Passenger/car ferries vary in size and capacity;
one of the largest in Europe is the British 11,500-
ton motor ship *Eagle* running between Southampton, Lisbon and Tangier, with space for 200
cars. On a much shorter daily cross-channel
route, one of the recent Thoresen ships can carry
320 cars and 1,200 passengers at a speed of 21
knots. Similar vessels operate in the Baltic and
in the Mediterranean where one of the latest, the
8,000-ton *Dana Corona*, has cabin accommodation
for 600 passengers and drive-on/drive-off facilities
for 150 cars on a weekly service between Italy and
Spain. Within the British Isles there are many
passenger/car ferries not only across to the
Continent and Ireland, but also in the Clyde
estuary, from the mainland of Scotland to the
Western Isles, Orkney and Shetland. With so
many ferries in these and similar waters, used by
thousands of holidaymakers, this type of ship is
now very familiar.

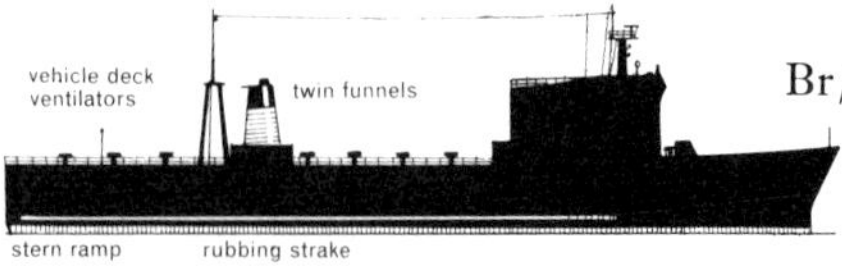

vehicle deck ventilators • twin funnels

MV *Domino*
Br/1971/1,582 gt/
108·22 m/17 k
Fig. 59

stern ramp • rubbing strake

RO/RO unit load ship

The drawing of a roll-on/roll-off cargo vessel
shows some of the features in which it differs from
the passenger/car ferry. A hydraulically operated
stern ramp—capable of taking a load of 70 tonnes
—gives container lorries direct access to the main
deck and a 30-tonne truck lift enables some of the
lorries and containers to be raised to the shelter
deck. The overall capacity of the ship is for 185
standard 6·09-metre containers. If conventionally
packed, or crated, cargo is delivered at the quayside
and can be packed in containers before shipment.
Some units are conveyed on road transport
vehicles and therefore accommodation is provided
for twelve lorry drivers.

This particular twin-screw vessel has no cargo-
handling gear as this is unnecessary for the type
of cargo she carries. Similar ships equipped as
multi-purpose vessels do have derricks or deck
cranes. The large number of mushroom ventilators provide air to the container decks.

Fig. 60   MV *Skyway* Br/1968/
1,279 gt/92·01 m/15 k

Fig. 61 MV *Anderida* Br/1971/ 1,601 gt/105·98 m/17 k *By courtesy of British Rail*

This ship is similar to **Fig. 60** and fulfils the same function except that she has a rail deck. She carries freight wagons on the Dover/Dunkerque route. As well as the normal short-sea vessel's rubbing strake, she has extra projections forward to assist docking at the rail terminal. She has bow, stern and side loading doors.

Fig. 62 MV *Horsa* Br/1972/ 5,000 gt/117·30 m/19·5 k *By courtesy of British Rail*

This is a multi-purpose ship operated between Folkestone and Boulogne, Calais and Ostend with space for 1,400 passengers and 210 cars or 38 commercial vehicles. She has the high freeboard, long superstructure and lack of derricks typical of the present-day version of the cross-channel packet. The large funnel has an additional structure to carry the exhaust gases well clear of the passenger decks.

Fig. 63
MV
Saint-Germain
Fr/1951/
3,094 gt/
115·80 m/
16·5 k

By courtesy of British Rail

Train ferry

In appearance, the train ferry does not differ very much from the RO/RO passenger/car ferry. The comparatively broad beam, high freeboard, lack of derricks, stern port and lack of sheer are features common to both types. Exceptions are some of the large train ferries running across the southern Baltic, which are much more like versions of passenger liners. The essential part of the train ferry is the long continuous main deck, which may be fitted with four tracks, giving a total of up to 360 metres of rails. Access to this rail deck is through a stern, or bow port over a link span connecting the ship's rails to the terminal rail tracks (**Fig. 63**).

Ferries carrying passengers are equipped with dining saloons and other public rooms, and therefore have many more portholes, side windows and lifeboats, and greater promenade space than the freight train only ferry. The upper drawing **a** shows a modern ship which carries passengers, cars and railway wagons between Kristiansand in southern Norway and Denmark. Other ferries ply between Denmark and Germany, e.g. MV *Danmark* (1968/6,300 gt) with accommodation for twelve railway coaches, wagons, road vehicles, and 1,500 passengers. MV *Sassnitz* (1958/6,164 gt) serves a similar role between Sweden and East Germany.

A daily through passenger train runs from London to Paris and Brussels via Dover/Dunkerque. From Harwich to Zeebrugge (or Dunkerque), four ships like drawing **b**, run a freight only service for 35 wagons on four recessed rail tracks.

Other, mainly freight only, train ferries with similar characteristic features, include those which operate between: Denmark and Sweden, Sweden and Finland, the mainland of Italy and Messina; there are also six inter-island services in Japan. In eastern Canada train ferries connect New Brunswick with Newfoundland and, south of the Great Lakes is a system of non-self-propelled freight wagon ferries between Detroit, Michigan and Windsor.

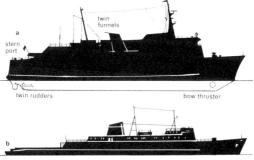

Fig. 64 **a** MV *Christian IV*
No/1968/2,708 gt/87·12 m/19 k
b MV *Cambridge Ferry*
Br/1963/3,294 gt/123·72 m/13·5 k

Estuarial ferry

Passenger and car ferries operating in comparatively sheltered waters vary a good deal in size and in general appearance. Some of them resemble the RO/RO short-sea ferries already illustrated, while others are not much more than self-propelled double-ended pontoons. Similarly, the time spent on passage can vary from a few minutes to perhaps one hour or more.

Fig. 65   MV *Glen Sannox*
Br/1957/1,107 gt/78·33 m/18 k

This is a twin-screw passenger/car ferry, with side and stern loading doors, operating on the Firth of Clyde. She is seen here on the twenty-minute passage between Gourock and Dunoon.

Fig. 66   Vehicle ferry *Sound of Islay*
Br/1968/280 gt/43·28 m/10·75 k

Fig. 67   MV *Royal Daffodil*
Br/1958/609 gt/48·46 m/12 k

The *Sound of Islay* makes short runs between islands in the Inner Hebrides. This twin-screw motor vessel has stern loading, a very chunky bridge set almost in the bows, and two side funnels much further aft which are not at first recognized as funnels.   In the photograph, at Rothesay, she is loaded with skips of bricks and the stern ramp is raised.

Six passenger only ferries give an almost continuous shuttle service across the River Mersey between Liverpool and Birkenhead and Wallasey. **Fig. 67** shows a twin-screw ferry designed with a rather large superstructure to operate only in sheltered waters.   As she must carry a maximum of 1,950 passengers in all weathers, they must all be provided with shelter for the ferry passage although it is of only a few minutes' duration.

In all parts of the world where thousands of daily commuters must cross from one city to an adjacent one, or from one part of a city to another, there are variations on the passenger ferry.   The less sheltered the waters, and the longer the passage, the more the ferry will have a shiplike appearance.

Fig. 68

PS *Waverley*
Br/1947/
693 gt/75·63m/
SR/14 k

Paddle steamer

After a history of more than a century and a half
the paddle steamer has now become a museum
piece.   In her later days she was represented only
by two categories of vessel—tugs and excursion
vessels operating in sheltered waters.   The side
paddles enabled the ship to make quick turns and
rapid manoeuvres alongside piers, particularly in
strong currents.   This great advantage is now
obtained by the use of Voith–Schneider propellers
and bow thruster units (page 17).   The excursion
paddle steamer was always distinctive with her
slender funnels, sharply raked masts, light superstructure and semi-circular paddle boxes, often
decorated in colour and gold leaf.   Many of the
steamers were able to accommodate about two
thousand passengers on day excursions.

   The last—and only—seagoing paddle steamer of
this type still running is the *Waverley*, owned by
Caledonian MacBrayne Ltd and used for summer
excursions in the Clyde estuary and among the
adjoining islands.   The same company runs the
Maid of the Loch (1953) on Loch Lomond during

the summer months. Only just in time, before the final disappearance of this attractive type of ship, groups of enthusiasts have made successful attempts to preserve a few of the survivors. Founded in 1959 the Paddle Steamer Preservation Society later acquired the last of the River Dart passenger paddle steamers, with the intention of running her themselves during the summer. Some of the last paddle steamers have been preserved as floating restaurants or club houses. The *Ryde* (ex-British Rail ferry of 1937), *Caledonia* (1934) from the Clyde and the Red Funnel paddler *Princess Elizabeth* (1927) are all in this category.

A few paddle tugs have been successfully saved from the ship breakers. The steam tug *Eppleton Hall* (1914) recently made a remarkable 10,000-mile, six-month voyage from England to San Francisco, to her museum resting-place alongside the restored Scottish sailing ship *Balclutha*. The *John H. Amos* (1931) has been acquired by the Teesside Museum, and the Maritime Trust has purchased the *Reliant* (1907) for preservation in the National Maritime Museum at Greenwich.

Two steam paddle ferries still ply on the Humber and are likely to do so until the completion of the new road bridge, and there is some hope that one of these vessels will be preserved. As recently as the 1950s paddle tugs were built for the Royal Navy for work in the naval dockyards. They are diesel-electric vessels with twin funnels placed abreast. Of the many large, and very decorative, stern-wheel paddlers formerly running on the Mississippi, and other North American rivers, the last survivor was the *Delta Queen*, registered at Cincinnati, and employed on excursions of several days' length between New Orleans and Memphis.

Fig. 69

Motor Tug *MSC Ulex* Br/1965/127 gt/1,300 hp*
A Manchester Ship Canal Company tug manoeuvring the Finnish cargo liner *Hansa* /1961/ OSD/CSD/ 6030/8,796 gt/ 148 m/15 k

Fig. 70

Motor Tug *Gannet* Br/ 1967/143 gt/ 1,200 hp

Slightly larger than the *MSC Ulex*, this harbour tug is propelled by two Voith-Schneider units. Unlike the other two tugs, she has the towing hook close to the stern and lacks the usual towbeams.

Fig. 71

Motor Tug *Flying Falcon* Br/1968/213 gt/1,470 hp/ 12·5 k

Propelled by a Kort nozzle unit, this vessel is equipped for fire-fighting duties, particularly at oil instal- lations, in the Clyde area.

* Horse-power (hp) to be replaced by kW metric units.

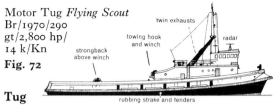

Motor Tug *Flying Scout*
Br/1970/290
gt/2,800 hp/
14 k/Kn
Fig. 72

strongback above winch

towing hook and winch

twin exhausts

radar

rubbing strake and fenders

Tug

Whatever her size, the tug can rarely be mistaken for any other type of vessel. She has high bows, a short superstructure set far forward, and the funnel (or twin funnels) and mast close to the wheelhouse. The fixed or spring-loaded towing hook is at the after end of the superstructure and, so that the towline does not foul the after-deck fittings, they are protected by transverse, curved steel hoops known as towbeams or strongbacks. Many of the newest motor tugs have twin exhausts incorporated in the mast structure. The tug's engines need to be very powerful and, to increase her manoeuvrability, the controllable pitch propeller and Kort nozzle are now commonly fitted; some tugs have Voith–Schneider units instead of the conventional propellers. Two-speed gear gives greater accuracy of control at low speeds, particularly against strong tides.

Every port has at least one tug equipped with fire-fighting apparatus, which consists of foam and fire monitors working from a platform on the mast. American tugs—known as towboats—differ in appearance from the normal European vessel, as regulations for crew accommodation result in a longer superstructure. Moreover, these tugs usually push and nose ships about harbours instead of towing them. Many of the river tugs, generally handling a string of barges, are built with a flat stem and projecting 'buffers' for pushing.

Salvage tug

The ocean-going salvage tug is the largest of the family and she may be employed in towing a floating dock halfway round the world, or an oil rig from shipyard to drilling station. But most of her time is spent patrolling the international shipping lanes, just waiting for a distress signal. When this is received the tug, and others who have heard the signal, race to the disabled ship to compete for the salvage work. A Dutch company

Fig. 73

Salvage Tug *Uragan* USSR/1961/1,151 gt/61·00 m/17k

has long dominated this field, but three giant German tugs are now available, and a new addition is the British *Lloydsman*. This very powerful tug is capable of towing the largest VLCC at 7 knots and she has a speed of 18·5 knots when running free. The *Lloydsman* gains much of her efficiency and power from a controllable pitch propeller in a Towmaster 5·2–metre diameter Kort nozzle with aerofoil steering vanes (see **Fig. 5**). As well as a wide range of salvage equipment, which includes two 10–tonne derricks, this tug is equipped with three foam and water fire monitors on the foremast. She has two tall buff funnels set athwartships, with a mast rising from them.

Fig. 74

MV *Lloydsman* Br/1971/2,041 gt 80·40m/ 16,000 hp/18 k

By courtesy of United Towing Co. Ltd

Fig. 75 MV *Majestic Service*
Br/1971/692 gt/
56·22 m

Oil rig supply vessel

This new type can be seen in various ports associated with underwater drilling for oil. She resembles a large tug—in fact towing is one of her
tasks—with the forward superstructure and clear
working deck aft. The main functions of the ship
are to carry stores, fuel oil, drilling water, cement,
drilling gear and personnel to the offshore rigs, and
to tow the rigs themselves to new stations and to
handle their heavy anchor gear. All this work

Fig. 76
MV *Smit-Lloyd*
11 Ne/1971/
744 gt/ 52·70 m/
3 k

may have to be done in extremely bad weather and,
therefore, the ships are seaworthy and powerful.
The cargo deck can be manoeuvred under the rig
platform for offloading pipes, casing and other
items. On some ships cylindrical cement tanks
are fixed at the forward end of the working deck,
and others are fitted with a mobile gantry crane
which runs the full length of this deck.

Fig. 77 *Sonda I* 1948/18,631 gt/194·40 m

Oil drilling vessel

With the rapid and extensive increase in the number of underwater oilfields in various parts of the world, some new types of ships have evolved. Many of the huge drilling platforms bear no resemblance whatsoever to a ship (**Fig. 78**) but some purpose-built and converted ships are in use. The drawing shows such a conversion from a Norwegian whale oil factory ship. Some of the original features typical of the factory do remain, but the obvious additions are the 60–metre drilling derrick and the helicopter platform.

A drilling ship must have powerful anchoring gear at the bows and stern to enable her to remain stationary against the forces of heavy seas, strong currents, long period swell and strong winds. Some of the purpose-built ships have a large rect-angular well under the derrick through which the drill passes to the sea-bed, while on other ships the drilling operations are done outboard on a cantilevered platform. Other features of the drilling vessel are large racks for stowage of standard lengths of drill pipe and oil-field casing, and a laboratory for the study of drill cores. Non-visible features include large tanks for carriage of liquid and bulk mud, bulk cement, drilling and potable water, and oil fuel. Diesel-electric units usually supply power for the underwater drilling and the auxiliary equipment. The French *Pelican* (1972) has a similar profile to **Fig. 77**, but a smaller superstructure aft.

By courtesy of P & O

Fig. 78 Supply vessel *Lady Margaret* 1968/480 gt/50·40 m/3,000 hp/2,250 kW/12k

The supply, anchor handling and towing vessel close to the BP oil rig *Sea Quest*, in the Firth of Forth, where she has been towed for the renewal of the rig's anchor wires. The *Lady Margaret* is owned by a consortium of P & O and French, Dutch and Norwegian interests. She can carry up to 700 tonnes of drilling gear and has accommodation for twelve passengers.

Fig. 79

Navigation buoys on the foredeck of a Northern Lighthouse Commission tender at Granton about to leave on a four-day servicing voyage

Lighthouse tender

The lighthouse tender is a small vessel with a long superstructure and generally has a smart and well cared for appearance. The two main functions are firstly, to service navigation buoys and secondly, to carry relief crews and supplies to lighthouses on island and rock stations, and lightships. For the former purpose the ship is equipped with a heavy derrick on the foremast, so that buoys can be lifted out of the water and placed on the foredeck.

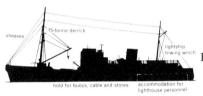

sheaves
15-tonne derrick
lightship towing winch
hold for buoys, cable and stores
accommodation for lighthouse personnel

Fig. 80

Trinity House tender *Siren*
Br/1960/1,425 gt/
67·35 m/DE(2)/
13 k

Some vessels like the cable ship (page 74) have sheaves fitted on the stem—a feature also found on Ministry of Defence buoy and net-laying vessels.

Navigation buoys and lights in England and Wales are under the general authority of Trinity House; those in Scotland and the Isle of Man are under the Commissioners of Northern Lights. Those in Eire are under the Commissioners of Irish Lights. The flags worn by ships under these authorities are shown in **Fig. 108**. Some of the large estuaries, such as the Firth of Clyde, are under separate navigation authorities who are responsible for all buoys and navigation lights.

The lightship is, in Great Britain, a non-self-propelled vessel which is anchored in a permanent position. It has a crew on board who attend to the light, fog signals and radio equipment. This type of vessel is now being replaced by an automatic, unmanned floating beacon.

*By courtesy of the
Meteorological Office*

Weather ship

A weather ship is an ocean-going vessel which remains on station for the purpose of making day and night meteorological observations to be sent back by radio to a land forecasting office. On the North Atlantic there are nine weather stations manned by ships provided by the United States and five European countries, including four vessels belonging to Great Britain. In addition to obtaining and reporting observations on weather conditions, some work is done on oceanography for various institutions. Each ship is also well equipped with air/sea rescue facilities.

Ships vary in size, but all have the latest forms of radar, radio, radio-communication systems and navigational aids; all reporting is done in an international figure code. The British ships are converted *Castle* class frigates propelled by steam reciprocating engines and oil-fired water-tube boilers. As the weather ships are stationed in waters too deep for anchoring, they must continue steaming to keep on station and fuel consumption is, therefore, very high. The British ships remain at sea for 24 days before returning to their home port of Greenock. For easy visibility the funnel and upperworks of a weather ship are painted orange on a grey hull.

Fig. 81 SS *Weather Monitor*
Br/1944/1,405 disp/76·77 m/SR/16·5 k

Cable ship

The earlier steam cable layers were very yacht-like in appearance, and even contemporary motor vessels have retained something of the same character. The deeply curved clipper stem, with sheaves and gantry, is the most obvious feature, and the long superstructure, many portholes, and several lifeboats all indicate a large complement of crew and cable engineers. Cable layers are generally within the range of 5/6,000 gross tons.

The function of this type of ship is either to lay new telephone cable (which is about 30 mm in diameter) or to inspect and repair existing cable. New cable is paid out over the stern sheaves from huge vertical tanks which can hold up to 3,000 kilometres of cable. Existing cable is grappled for over the bow sheaves, inspected, and repaired as required before it is returned to the sea-bed. The cable ship must be easily manoeuvrable so she is

twin funnels

helicopter platform

bow gantry and sheaves

crane

active rudder   cable tanks   bow thruster

Fig. 82

British PO cable ship, 1973/3,500 disp/94·50 m/M

fitted with a bow thruster and, as in the case of the ship illustrated, with an activated rudder and controllable pitch propeller. The drawing shows the profile of two new ships equipped for shallow and deep-water work in any part of the world from the Arctic to the Tropics. They incorporate a new system of pan loading in which the cables are loaded in very large containers—like giant cassettes. Some other examples of cable ships are: *Mercury* (Cable & Wireless), *Alert* (UK PO), *Long Lines* USA and *Ingul* USSR.

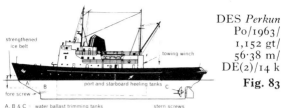

DES *Perkun*
Po/1963/
1,152 gt/
56·38 m/
DE(2)/14 k

Fig. 83

A, B & C = water ballast trimming tanks   stern screws

Icebreaker

In Canada, Russia and the Baltic many ferries and other craft have hulls which are strengthened for navigation in ice, but harbour and seagoing ice-breakers are specially constructed to clear passages for others. The all-welded hull is different from any other type of vessel. So that the cleared passage is wide enough for the following ships, the icebreaker's beam must be a metre or so wider than theirs and, to give the maximum man-oeuvrability her own length must be comparatively short; therefore the beam-length ratio is about 1:5. The drawing shows the deeply-cut stem that enables the icebreaker to ride up onto the ice and crush it by sheer weight, which is increased when water ballast is pumped into the forward trimming tanks. Side trimming tanks are used to give a rocking or heeling motion. The hull plating is strengthened at the water-line by a 6–metre band with a thickness of between 30 and 50 millimetres. The rounded section of the ship's sides—known as the tumblehome—helps to force her upwards in reaction to the side pressure from the ice. The Russian *Lenin*, built in 1959, is a huge triple-screw icebreaker propelled by turbo-electric nuclear power. She has a length of 134 metres to a beam of 27·63 metres; running free she can maintain a speed of eighteen knots.

Fig. 84 *Arabatskiy*
USSR/1966/1,972 gt/

Trailing suction dredger 81·94 m/DE(2)

The seagoing suction dredger is an engines aft vessel not unlike the coastal tanker in profile, but distinguishable by the much greater complexity of the gear between the forecastle and the navigating bridge.   This gear consists of a horizontal suction, or drag pipe, suction pipe hoisting machinery and boom, and discharge gear for operating the hopper bottom doors.   During dredging operations the suction pipe is trailed along the sea-bed and the spoil is pumped into the hopper.   When this is full, the ship steams out to the dumping ground and the spoil is discharged by gravity, or it may be pumped ashore for land reclamation. Another form of suction dredger (**Fig. 85**) is used to dredge marketable sand and gravel for building and civil engineering purposes.   It works like the harbour-deepening dredge, but the cargo is discharged ashore at special wharves.

Fig. 85

MV *Norstar*
Br/1961/614 gt/
47·54 m/9 k

A sand and gravel suction dredger returning to port with her cargo

Fig. 86 SS *Shieldhall* Br/1955/
1,792 gt/81·86 m/SR(2)

Sludge disposal vessel

The sludge vessel may be seen in most estuaries associated with large centres of population such as the Thames, Clyde or the Mersey. Full treatment of sewage results in large quantities of sludge, which is pumped from the sewage works to the disposal vessel's tanks. This is then conveyed out to sea to specific dumping grounds and discharged by gravity. The drawing shows a modern vessel owned by the Corporation of Glasgow. The ship is propelled by twin diesel engines and a controllable pitch propeller and Kort nozzle unit, and a bow thruster to assist her in turning in narrow waters close to the loading berth.

Fig. 87

MV *Dalmarnock*
Br/1970/2,050 gt/
95·11 m/11·5 k

The *Dalmarnock* might be mistaken for a coastal tanker but for the three large ventilators. On her daily voyage with 3,000 tonnes of sludge she takes about four hours to reach the dumping grounds. Another ship belonging to the same authority (**Fig. 86**) has a long superstructure which makes classification difficult; she can accommodate parties of passengers during the summer months.

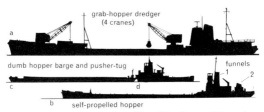

grab-hopper dredger
(4 cranes)

a

dumb hopper barge and pusher-tug

funnels
1
2

c

d

b

self-propelled hopper

Fig. 88 Port of London
dredging craft

Grab dredger and hopper

In its simplest form the grab dredger is a pontoon
with a slewing and hoisting crane capable of
operating a double-chain grab.   Many improvised
craft are like this, but others have a seaworthy hull
and propelling machinery.   The grab dredger has
an advantage over the bucket dredger in docks and
basins, as it can work in awkward corners.   The
spoil may be either transferred directly to a hopper
alongside or, if the craft is self-propelled, carried
to the dumping grounds out at sea, or, alternatively
discharged at a land reclamation unit.   The drawings show some examples of seagoing craft built in
the 1960s.   Drawing **a** is the *Long Reach* with a
length of 80·41 metres capable of carrying 2,000
tonnes of spoil.   This twin-screw, twin-rudder,
grab hopper is powered by three-cylinder steam
engines.   Her four steam grabs each have a
capacity of 2·832 m³ and can work to depths
of over 15 metres.   **b** is a self-propelled self-
discharging motor hopper with a twin rudder-
propeller unit and a length of 63·63 metres.   She
has an unusual arrangement of three funnel exhausts.   The dumb hopper (**c**), as the name implies,
has no propelling machinery and it is necessary for
her to be either towed, or pushed out to the spoil
grounds by a tug.   Her spoil is discharged by
gravity through bottom-opening doors.

Bucket ladder dredger

The bucket ladder dredger has no hopper space, so the spoil must be transferred to hopper barges alongside. It may or may not be self-propelled. The hull has an open well through which the ladder can be lowered to a depth that may be down to 21

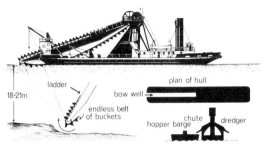

Fig. 89 The working of a bucket dredger

metres. The endless belt of buckets, each with a capacity of 0·5 to 0·7 m³, moves round and, as each bucket reaches the bottom, it scoops up some spoil and carries it to the top of the ladder. A tripping device tips the bucket and empties the spoil into a chute down into the hopper barge.

Fig. 90 Twin-screw motor bucket ladder *Blythswood* Br/ 1963/786 gt/64·00 m working on the River Clyde

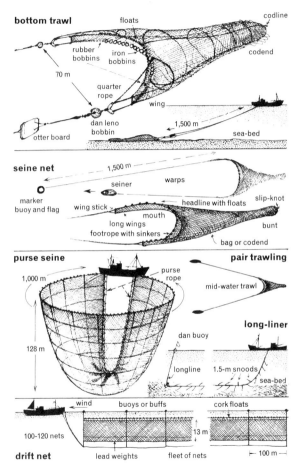

bottom trawl
floats
codline
rubber bobbins
iron bobbins
codend
70 m
quarter rope
codend
wing
otter board
dan leno bobbin
1,500 m
sea-bed

seine net
1,500 m
seiner
warps
marker buoy and flag
wing stick
headline with floats
slip-knot
mouth
long wings
footrope with sinkers
bunt
bag or codend

purse seine
1,000 m
purse rope
128 m

pair trawling
mid-water trawl

long-liner
dan buoy
longline
1.5-m snoods
sea-bed

wind
buoys or buffs
cork floats
100–120 nets
13 m
drift net
lead weights
fleet of nets
100 m

Fig. 91 Methods of fishing

3 FISHING VESSELS

Methods of Fishing

Trawling The bottom trawl is a large conical bag of net which is dragged along the sea-bed to catch demersal fish such as cod, plaice and haddock. The mouth of the net is held open by the kite-like action of the two otter boards. The lighter mid-water floating trawl—without ground bobbins—is towed by one, or a pair of trawlers to catch non-bottom feeding, or pelagic, fish such as herring, mackerel and sprats. **Seining** (pronounced *see-ning*). The seine net is also conical but has neither ground bobbins nor otter boards. The two long warps, and the net, are paid out in the form of a triangle, and, when the boat returns to its marker buoy, the net is drawn in with its catch of flatfish, cod and haddock. **Purse seining,** similar to Scottish pair boat ring-netting, has grown rapidly in recent years with the development of large, light, nylon nets and the power block. The huge net is shot in an arc and the two ends gradually drawn together to enclose the shoal in the bag, or purse. The purse-rope is drawn in and the bag reduced in size until the catch is brought alongside in the bunt. This method is widely used for catching herring, pilchard, sardine, sardinella, anchoveta, mackerel and tuna. **Long-lining** is used to catch haddock, ling and cod where the sea-bed is rocky and uneven. The hundreds of hooks are baited with pieces of herring or mussel. **Drifting** The drift net consists of a meshed screen of gillnets several kilometres in length in which the herring and other pelagic fish are caught by their gills. This traditional, passive form of fishing—employed at night when the fish feed nearer the surface—is being replaced by less arduous active methods of purse seining and mid-water trawling.

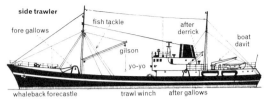

side trawler

fore gallows

fish tackle

after derrick

boat davit

gilson

yo-yo

whaleback forecastle   trawl winch   after gallows

Fig. 92 Deep-sea side trawler for middle-water fishing

Trawler

The trawler is engaged in all-the-year-round fishing, often in some of the stormiest waters in the world, and must therefore be a strong, sturdy vessel able to work in the worst of weather. The side trawler has a pronounced sheer, a superstructure placed well aft and a clear foredeck fitted with compartments, or fish pounds, for sorting the catch. During the towing operations the trawl-warps pass through pulleys in the fore, and aft, gallows. Some trawlers have these on the starboard side only and others on both sides. Another characteristic of the trawler is the powerful winch placed just forward of the wheelhouse. Present-day trawlers are well equipped with marine electronics, i.e. navigators, auto-pilots, radar and sonar equipment for fish locating. Three main categories of trawlers operate from British ports.

Fig. 93 Middle-water side trawler

Distant-water trawlers with lengths of 50/85 m fish, mainly for cod, in the Barents Sea, off Greenland, Iceland, Spitsbergen and Newfoundland, often making round voyages of up to 5,000 miles from the main ports of Hull, Grimsby and Fleetwood. *Middle-water trawlers*, with lengths of about 50 m, operate from Aberdeen, Granton and Fleetwood to Iceland, the North Cape and the White Sea. *Near-water trawlers* based on Aberdeen and Lowestoft are 30/40 m vessels mainly fishing in the North Sea, while a large number of smaller vessels take part in inshore fishing.

Stern Trawler

Great improvements were made in working conditions with the introduction of the stern trawler on which the net, with full codend, is hauled inboard through the stern slipway. When the codline is released the catch falls through a hatch to the lower deck where the crew are able to sort, gut and box the fish under cover. This type of trawler is easily distinguished from the conventional side trawler by the stern opening with gantry above and bipod or twin masts from which the derricks and net-handling gear are operated. Furthermore, the stern trawler usually has twin funnels either on the superstructure or separate from it, amidships.

Fig. 94

Stern Trawler built in 1971 with a length of 44·28 m

fishing lights

stern trawler

bipod mast

gantry

trawl deck

trawl winch

stern ramp

Freezer trawler and factory ship

On the normal trawler the crew wash and gut the
fish, and then pack it on ice in boxes, where it will
remain fresh for about fourteen days; the time
which a vessel can remain at sea is therefore
restricted by this limitation. The freezer trawler
can remain at sea for many weeks longer than this
as the catch is sorted, washed, gutted and then
frozen into about 40-kg blocks and retained at a
temperature of about $-28°C$, until port is reached.
The fish is then thawed out and either sold as
fresh fish or kept in storage. The fish factory
trawler carries the work a stage further while still
at sea. The catch is not only cleaned and gutted,

Fig. 95

Freezer factory
stern trawler

but also filleted, skinned and processed ready for
the market. This type of vessel must, therefore,
be larger to accommodate the extra machinery
refrigerating plant and processing machinery.
The greater part of the catch is treated in this way
while some is converted into liver oil; offal and
small fish are turned into fish meal. The illustration shows a French vessel with a large refrigerated hold, fish meal and fish oil tanks, a full
equipment of headers, filleters and skinners, fully
automatic freezing plant, a closed-circuit television
to monitor both the fishing operations on deck and
the processing below decks.

Fig. 96 Russian
stern-operating fish
factory, 3,050
gross tons

84

Scottish seiner

Fig. 97

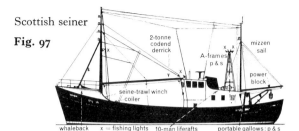

2-tonne codend derrick

A-frames p & s

mizzen sail

power block

x

seine-trawl winch coiler

whaleback   x = fishing lights   10-man liferafts   portable gallows: p & s

Seiner

Seine net fishing was first developed in Scandinavia before the last war. Used by Scottish fishermen during that period, its use has now become widespread. The seine net is shot, and hauled in, over the stern and it is necessary to have a clear space between the wheelhouse and the stern; this is, therefore, a characteristic feature of the seiner. As the warps are being hauled in they are passed forward to a machine, close to the foremast, which coils them neatly on each side of the deck. Both the coiler and the coiled warps can be seen in **Fig. 99***b*. The drawing shows the main characteristics of the Scottish seiner and, as this particular vessel is dual purpose, it has the addition of portable steel gallows on the port and starboard quarters for stern trawling. The hydraulic power block, a recent innovation, is now a common feature on even comparatively small fishing boats as it greatly facilitates the handling of the nets. The seiner/trawler shown in the drawing has a length of 22·86 m and a crew of eight. The steel hull has a cruiser stern, a soft-nosed stem and a prominent whaleback, which gives considerable shelter to the men operating the winch and the coiler. Instead of the traditional lifeboat, the vessel carries two of the new type of tenmen liferafts.

85

Fig. 98 Some British motor fishing vessels

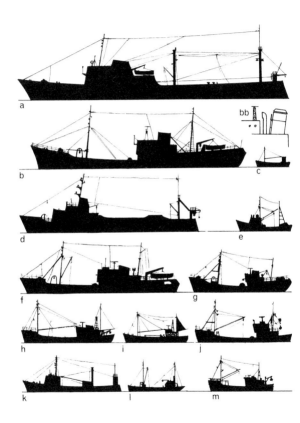

a Stern factory trawler, 1,435 g.r.t. with diesel-electric propulsion. **b Distant-water conventional side trawler**, 839 g.r.t. with diesel-electric propulsion and speed of 15 knots, crew of 42, 67 m o.a. In 1972 there were about sixty distant-water steam trawlers of the 1950s sailing from Hull and Grimsby. They can be distinguished by the cowl top funnel, steam pipe and engine-room ventilator **(bb)**. **c Small line and lobster boat**, 10 m o.a. **d Distant-water stern trawler**, fish-room capacity of 356 m³, crew of 16, 45 m o.a. **e Inshore stern trawler** with Kort nozzle rudder, 15·24 m o.a. **f Middle-water side trawler**, 280 g.r.t., 40 m o.a. **g Near-water 'pocket' side trawler**, 26·20 m o.a. **h Multi-purpose inshore boat** for pair trawling, side trawling and seining, 24·38 m o.a. **i Drifter** with wooden hull, mizzen sail and cage of floats, or pallets, and rollers along the bulwarks. **j Purse seiner** with power block, also equipped for stern and pair trawling, 26·51 m o.a **k Near-water stern trawler** with variable pitch propellor, 25 m o.a. **l Brixham trawler** with Rolls-Royce engine, 14 m o.a. **m Inshore multi-purpose fishing vessel** built in 1972 in Orkney and owned in Yorkshire. Glass fibre hull, 16·45 m o.a.

Fig. 99   *a* Drifter   *b* Deck of a seiner

Fig. 100 Some European fishing vessels

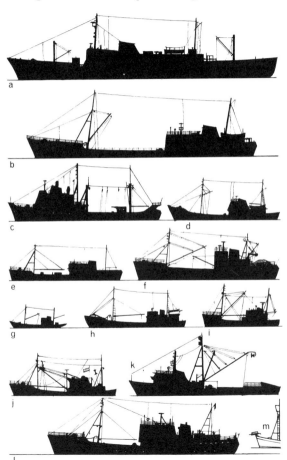

a Polish stern freezer trawler, crew of 93 and speed of 12·5 knots.   85 m o.a.   **b French deep-sea salt cod trawler** employed on three voyages a year to Newfoundland Banks. Diesel-electric propulsion.   68 m o.a.   **c Polish stern trawler** built in 1963.   48 m o.a.   **d Spanish pareja** with comparatively high freeboard and clear net platform aft, employed in pair fishing on Newfoundland Banks.   35 m o.a.   **e Faroese long liner**, crew of 24 on voyages of 10/12 days' duration laying baited line up to 50 km in length.   36 m o.a.   **f Norwegian purse seiner** with characteristic high poop and power block.   Frequently seen off Orkney and Shetland.   46 m o.a.   **g Portuguese sardine seiner** fishes in coastal waters on two-day trips.   18 m o.a.   **h Danish fishing cutter**, crew of six or seven.   A sturdy type of vessel capable of fishing in Barents Sea and off Greenland.   30 m o.a.   **i Dutch motor-fishing cutter** sometimes fitted with Kort nozzle.   24 m o.a.   **j Dutch nearwater fishing cutter** built in 1972.   32 m o.a.   **k Spanish tuna purse seiner,** 1972 with facilities for freezing catch.   45 m o.a.   **l Norwegian fisheries research trawler** with larger superstructure, and more accommodation, than commercial fishing trawler.   60 m o.a.   **m** Forepart of **Norwegian shark-fishing vessel** with harpoon gun on the stem and rope-ladder to crow's nest.

Fig. 101   *a* Norwegian   *b* Polish fisheries
purse seiner   research vessel

Fig. 102 Some non-European fishing vessels

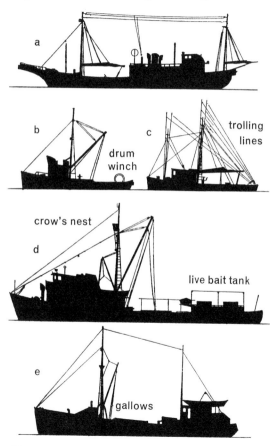

a

b

drum
winch

c

trolling
lines

crow's nest

d

live bait tank

e

gallows

The unusual looking vessel **a** is a modern Japanese mackerel pole and line fisherman. A continuous platform projects from the two sides of the ship right up to the overhanging clipper stem. Live bait is used and during the night fishing sessions powerful lights are hung over the side to attract the fish.

The smaller British Columbian fishing vessel **b** employs two methods of fishing: trolling from poles and lines attached to the foot of the mast and netting by means of a seine net handled over the stern by a powerful drum winch.

The **Pacific troller c** employs the trolling method with two or four rods and steel lines when fishing for salmon off the Pacific coast of North America. A similar method is used by the French tunnymen in the Bay of Biscay. Their rods, or tangons, are about 15 m in length and each one trails six to eight lines.

The **Tuna clipper d** is a 40-m flush-decked launch with a low freeboard used for tuna fishing off the west coast of Mexico, central America and south California. Individual fishermen, each with his own rod, hook and line, fish from a platform which projects all round the hull. Live bait is carried in tanks on the deck close to the stern.

The **New England trawler e** has a length of 23 m and a speed of 9 knots. Working off the eastern seaboard of North America, she makes about twenty trips each year fishing mainly for redfish.

All over the world there are numerous fishing fleets of varying types, but they tend to conform to the main categories already described. The method of fishing employed—whether trawling, drifting, ring netting, seining, long-lining, trolling or rod fishing—will determine their size and characteristics.

The whale factory ship

The **whale factory ship** is a large vessel with high freeboard, a navigating bridge placed well forward and a large superstructure aft with twin funnels. The stern slipway, through which the dead whales are hauled, leads to the flensing deck amidships. Here the carcass is stripped of blubber and cut up for disposal to various processing plants, either for retention as meat, or converted to oil, meat meal and other by-products. The whales are hunted, and harpooned by the small, fast whale catchers attendant on the 'mother' ship. They do duty as buoy boats and collect the dead whales together. Corvettes tow the whales to the factory ship. Modern whale factories are equipped with the latest electronic devices and some of them employ a helicopter for spotting the whales. One of the newest Russian ships is a 36,000 gross tons vessel capable of dealing with 4,000 whales each trip; it has accommodation for 650 crew and processing plant workers. The last British ship was disposed of in 1963 and a few years later the Norwegians—who pioneered many of the modern methods of whaling and dominated the industry for so long—also withdrew, leaving only the Japanese and the Russians to hunt for whales in the Antarctic. Their fleets leave home ports in October and spend the antarctic summer in the whaling grounds, returning home in the northern spring.

Fig. 103

The last Dutch whale factory now owned in South Africa and converted to a fish factory

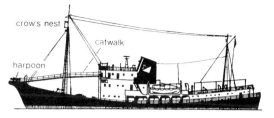

Fig. 104 Japanese whale catcher with crow's nest and catwalk, or gunner's bridge

---

SELECTION OF BRITISH AND IRISH PORT DISTINGUISHING LETTERS

A Aberdeen; AB Aberystwyth; AD Ardrossan; AH Arbroath; BCK Buckie; BF Banff; BM Brixham; C Cork; CF Cardiff; CK Colchester; CS Cowes; CT Castletown; CY Castlebay; D Dublin; DE Dundee; DH Dartmouth; DK Dundalk; DO Douglas; FD Fleetwood; FE Folkestone; FH Falmouth; FR Fraserburgh; FY Fowey; G Galway; GE Goole; GN Granton; GU Guernsey; GY Grimsby; H Hull; HH Harwich; HL Hartlepool; IE Irvine; INS Inverness; J Jersey; K Kirkwall; KY Kirkcaldy; LH Leith; LK Lerwick; LN King's Lynn; LT Lowestoft; LY Londonderry; M Milford Haven; NN Newhaven; OB Oban; PD Peterhead; PE Poole; PW Padstow; PGW Port Glasgow; PZ Penzance; R Ramsgate; RO Rothesay; S Skibbereen; SA Swansea; SC Scilly Isles; SE Salcombe; SH Scarborough; SN Shields, North; SR Stranraer; SS St Ives; SSS Shields, South; SY Stornoway; T Tralee; TH Teignmouth; TN Troon; UL Ullapool; W Waterford; WA Whitehaven; WD Wexford; WH Weymouth; WK Wick; WN Wigtown; WY Whitby; Y Yougal; YH Yarmouth.

Fig. 105 RS *Scotia*
Br/1971/1,521 gt/
68·6 m/DE/
14 k

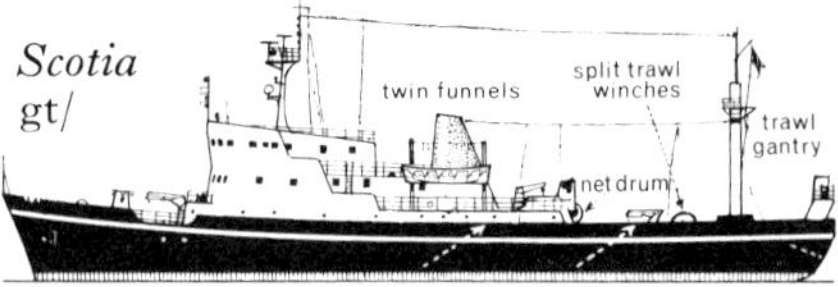

(labels on illustration: twin funnels, split trawl winches, trawl gantry, net drum, semi bulbous bow, laboratory, plankton crane, stern ramp)

Research ship

This stern-trawler type of vessel was built for the Department of Agriculture and Fisheries for Scotland. Its purpose was to engage in research in Greenland waters and the White Sea for the Marine Laboratory at Aberdeen. Accommodating twelve scientists, she is equipped with the latest gear, four laboratories, and deck machinery for deep water trawling. The RS *Cirolana*, based on Grimsby, undertakes similar work, while other ships study the middle and inshore fisheries. The much larger diesel-electric *Profesor Siedlecki* (1971/3,000 gt) (**Fig. 101** b) belongs to the Polish Fisheries Institute for research in a wide range of studies all over the world. Oceanological research ships are generally similar in appearance and are equipped with laboratories, scientific workshops, and core and hydrographic deck machinery to enable groups of scientists to spend periods at sea on geological, biological, magnetic or hydrographic research. The National Environment Research Council operates twenty ships. One, the Royal RS *Challenger*, has six laboratories, accommodation for nine scientists and a range of 2,600 nautical miles.

Fig. 106
RRS
Challenger
Br/1972/
1440 disp/
54·86 m/10·?

4 FLAGS

International Code (Plate 1)

The present version of the International Code of Signals came into being in 1934 and was revised in April 1969. The Royal Navy has its own code, although many of the same flags are used.

Signal letters

In addition to the letter values shown in **Plate 1**, each flag has a signal value. For example, the letter **D** also means 'Keep clear of me—I am manoeuvring with difficulty.' Every ship, and even many small yachts, has a four-letter identification signal. British ships have either **G** or **M** as the first letter. The letter **F** represents France, **PA** or **PI** Holland, and **K**, **N** or **W** the United States of America.

Every phrase likely to be used at sea is represented by a group of code letters. Each ship carries the official International Code books which contain all these recognized signals. If it is necessary to send an unusual signal, perhaps containing someone's name, the words may be spelt out letter by letter. To economize in flags, substitute flags are used; for instance, in the signal indicating the port of Plymouth, **AMPM**, the last letter would be indicated by a substitute flag instead of repeating the letter **M**.

Signals flags should always be flown from a point where they can be read without obstruction from masts or stays. If more than one point is used the signal reads from forward aft.

On festive occasions in port, ships of all types may 'dress ship', that is, fly all the code flags on a taut line hoisted from the stem or bowsprit over the trucks of the masts down to the stern.

Signal Flags: Selection of Signals

A I have a diver down; keep well clear at slow speeds. **B** I am taking in, or discharging, or carrying explosives. **C** Yes (*Affirmative*). **D** Keep clear of me—I am manoeuvring with difficulty. **E** I am altering my course to starboard. **F** I am disabled. **G** I require a pilot (for *Fishing Vessels*—I am hauling nets). **H** I have a pilot on board. **I** I am altering my course to port. **J** I am on fire and have dangerous cargo on board—keep well clear of me. **K** I wish to communicate with you. **L** You should stop your vessel instantly. **M** My vessel is stopped and making no way through the water. **N** No (*Negative*). **O** Man overboard. **P** (*Blue Peter*) *In harbour:* All persons are to repair on board as the vessel is about to proceed to sea (*flown at the foremast*). *At sea it may be used by fishing boats to mean:* My nets have come fast upon an obstruction. **Q** My vessel is healthy. I request a free pratique. (*A vessel arriving in British waters from abroad must declare whether she is 'Healthy' or 'Suspect'. Pratique is permission to hold intercourse with the port. If there is a case of infectious disease on board, the signal* **QQ** *is hoisted signifying* My ship is suspect.) **S** My engines are going astern. **T** Keep clear of me: I am engaged in pair trawling. **U** You are running into danger. **V** I require assistance. **W** I require medical assistance. **X** Stop carrying out your intentions and watch for my signals. **Y** I am dragging my anchor. **Z** I require a tug. *When made by fishing vessels operating in close proximity on the fishing-grounds* I am shooting nets. **Selection of two-letter signals: AM** Have you a doctor? **NC** I am in distress and require immediate assistance. Ships **GBTT** *Queen Elizabeth 2*, **FNRR** *France*, **GNVC** *Canberra*.

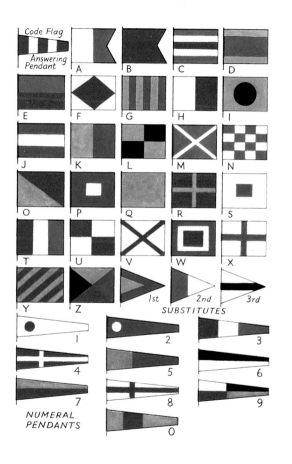

Plate I
International Code Flags (*see p. 95*)

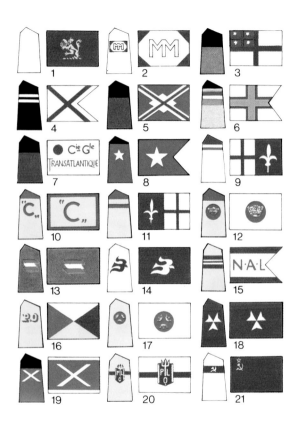

Plate 2
Colours of shipping companies
Passenger and Cruise Liners (*see p. 100*)

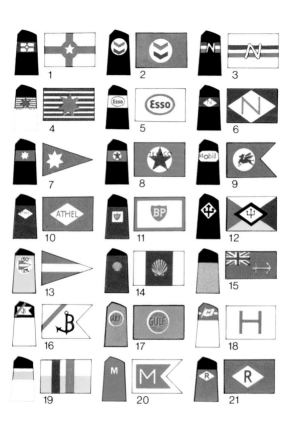

Plate 3
Colours of shipping companies
Tankers (*see p. 103*)

Plate 4
Colours of shipping companies
British Ocean-going Cargo Liners, Container Ships
and Bulk Carriers (1) (see p. 104)

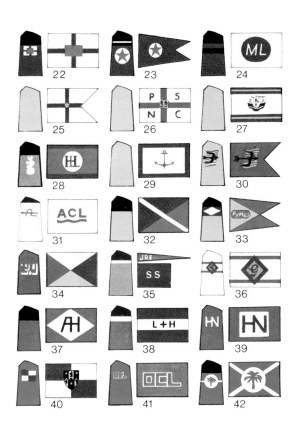

Plate 5
Colours of shipping companies
British Ocean-going Cargo Liners, Container Ships
and Bulk Carriers (2) (see p. 106)

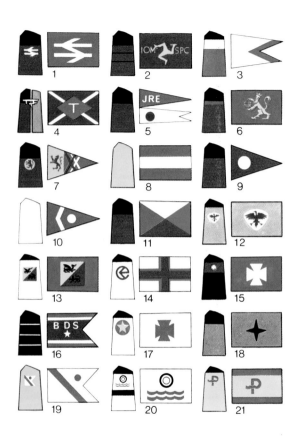

Plate 6
Colours of shipping companies
Passenger and Car Ferries within the British
Isles and to the Continent of Europe
(see p. 109)

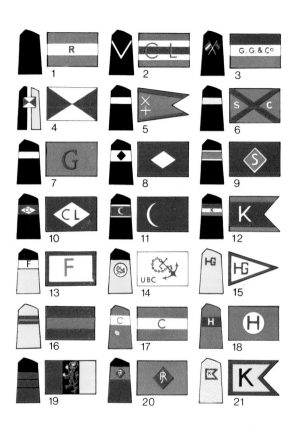

Plate 7
Colours of shipping companies
British Coaster and Home Trade (*see p. 111*)

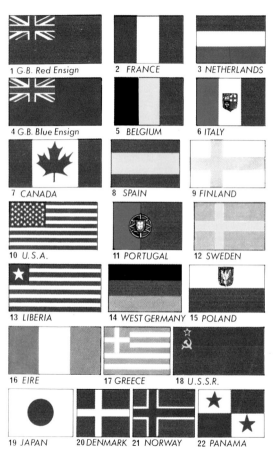

1 G.B. Red Ensign
2 FRANCE
3 NETHERLANDS
4 G.B. Blue Ensign
5 BELGIUM
6 ITALY
7 CANADA
8 SPAIN
9 FINLAND
10 U.S.A.
11 PORTUGAL
12 SWEDEN
13 LIBERIA
14 WEST GERMANY
15 POLAND
16 EIRE
17 GREECE
18 U.S.S.R.
19 JAPAN
20 DENMARK
21 NORWAY
22 PANAMA

Plate 8
Merchant Flags and Ensigns (see p. 97)

Merchant Flags (Plate 8 and Fig. 108)

Countries and governments are represented by national flags, and in many instances the merchant flag, worn by all types of merchant ship and pleasure craft, is identical. The merchant flag is worn at a vessel's stern on the ensign staff and is frequently referred to as an ensign. In port, merchant flags are hoisted at 8 a.m. between March and September, and at 9 a.m. between September and March; they are hauled down at sunset. They must be worn when a ship is entering or leaving port at any time of the day or night. British ships of over fifty tons are compelled by law to carry or wear their national merchant flags. **Fig. 107** shows the position at which various flags are worn.

British Ensigns

The RED ENSIGN (**Pl. 8** No. 1) is the flag of the Merchant Navy worn by all British-owned mer-

Fig. 107   Positions of flags worn by merchant ships and warships

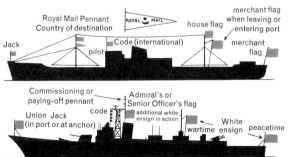

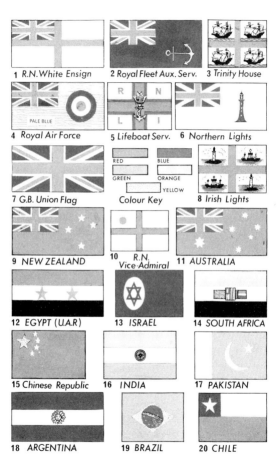

1 R.N. White Ensign   **2** Royal Fleet Aux. Serv.   **3** Trinity House

4 Royal Air Force   **5** Lifeboat Serv.   **6** Northern Lights

PALE BLUE

7 G.B. Union Flag   Colour Key   **8** Irish Lights

RED   BLUE   GREEN   ORANGE   YELLOW

9 NEW ZEALAND   **10** R.N. Vice-Admiral   **11** AUSTRALIA

12 EGYPT (U.A.R)   **13** ISRAEL   **14** SOUTH AFRICA

15 Chinese Republic   **16** INDIA   **17** PAKISTAN

18 ARGENTINA   **19** BRAZIL   **20** CHILE

Fig. 108 Merchant flags and ensigns

chant, pleasure or private craft.   The BLUE ENSIGN (**Pl. 8** No. 4) is worn as the merchant flag by British ships having among their crew a certain number of officers and men belonging to the Royal Naval Reserve.   Many yacht clubs use it defaced by their club emblems.   Lloyd's, Customs, and some other institutions also wear this flag with their badges in the fly, and the Royal Army Service Corps vessels wear a blue ensign with crossed swords.   The WHITE ENSIGN (**Fig. 108** No. 1) is the ensign of the Royal Navy and is worn by all HM ships, shore establishments and boats of the Royal Yacht Squadron.   Ships of the ROYAL FLEET AUXILIARY SERVICE wear a blue ensign defaced by a gold anchor (**Fig. 108** No. 2). ROYAL AIR FORCE stations, air sea rescue launches and other vessels use a pale blue ensign with the well-known roundel (**Fig. 108** No. 4).   Lifeboat stations fly the flag of the ROYAL NATIONAL LIFEBOAT INSTITUTION (**Fig. 108** No. 5) and the lifeboats wear a red ensign with a small version of the flag on the fly.   Lighthouse tenders in Scotland and the Isle of Man belonging to the COMMISSIONERS OF NORTHERN LIGHTS wear a blue ensign, but when the commissioners are on board a tender a white ensign (**Fig. 108** No. 6) is worn.   UNION FLAG (**Fig. 108** No. 7) is worn at the jackstaff of British warships at anchor or alongside a quay.   The pilot flag is a Union flag with a white border, known as the Union Jack, and worn at the jackstaff by merchant ships, or at the foremast when a pilot is required.   The Union flag is quite commonly, but incorrectly, referred to as the *Union Jack*.   **Fig. 108** No. 10 shows the Royal Navy COMMAND flag flown by a Vice-Admiral.

Flags of Convenience A number of merchant ships are now registered under the flags of Liberia (**Pl. 8** No. 13), Panama (**Pl. 8** No. 22) Honduras and Costa Rica.

COLOURS OF SHIPPING COMPANIES

The coloured plates show a selection of funnels and house flags grouped according to the major activity of the companies concerned.   Information in the text is arranged as follows: number of relevant illustration; name of company (i.e. English form followed by the official form unless it resembles the English); port of registry; classification of ships' names; hull colours, i.e. topsides/boot-topping; principal service routes or other information.

Passenger and Cruise Liners (Plate 2)

Some of the major companies with one or more vessels of about 15,000 gross tons, or over, operating passenger and/or cruise services.   Many of the companies also operate general cargo, bulk and oil carriers.
1 CUNARD LINE LTD, Liverpool. *Queen Elizabeth 2* and *Cunard*—. Grey/orange, or white/red. Southampton–Le Havre–New York. World-wide and Caribbean cruising. Also cargo and container ships.   On 20th April each year the old White Star company flag is worn with the normal house flag. **2** CIE DES MESSAGERIES MARITIMES, Paris. Various names. Black with white line/red, or white/green. World-wide services including large fleet of cargo liners with black funnels. **3** SHAW SAVILL LINE (Furness Withy Group) Southampton. Mainly names ending in *ic*. Black, grey or white/red. Same funnels as No. 34. UK to Australia and New Zealand. Cruising. Also fleet of cargo liners. **4** BRITISH INDIA STEAM NAVIGATION CO. LTD (P & O Passenger Division), London.

Eastern names ending in *a*. Black with white line/red, or white hulls. Mediterranean and Baltic educational cruises. Cargo and passenger-cargo liners. **5** UNION-CASTLE MAIL SS CO. LTD, London. — *Castle*. Lilac grey/brown. Southampton–South Africa, and cruising. Subsidiary of British and Commonwealth Shipping Group and therefore ships wear additional burgee above the company's own house flag. **6** SOUTH AFRICAN MARINE CORPORATION LTD, Cape Town. *SA* —. Grey or white/red or green. Operates similar service to, and in conjunction with, No. 5. **7** FRENCH LINE (Compagnie Générale Transatlantique), Le Havre. Various names. Black/red with white line. Europe to USA and Central and South America. **8** ACHILLE LAURO, Naples. — *Lauro* and various names. White, black or blue hulls. Europe to Australia and Mediterranean services. Cruising. **9** ITALIA LINE (Italia Societa per Azioni di Navigazione), Genoa. Names of prominent Italians of the past. Black with white line, or white with green line. Italy to North, Central and South America. Cruising. **10** COSTA LINE (Costa Armatori S.p.A- 'Linea C'), Genoa. Personal names and capital letter *C*. White with blue line/blue. Mediterranean to West Indies and South America. Cruising. **11** LLOYD TRIESTINO, Trieste. Names of prominent Italians. White with blue line/red or black. Mediterranean to Africa and Far East. **12** HOME LINES INC., Panama. —*ic*. White/ green. Cruising from Central America. **13** HOLLAND AMERICA LINE (Nederlandsche-Amerikaansche Stoomv. Maats), Rotterdam. Passenger liners: —*dam*. Cargo liners: —*dyk*. Black or grey/red. Europe to Canada, USA and Gulf ports. World-wide cruising. **14** ROYAL

VIKING LINE, Oslo. *Royal Viking* —. Owned by consortium of Norwegian shipowners. Cruising. **15** NORWEGIAN AMERICA LINE (Den Norske Amerikalinje A/S), Oslo. *—fjord*. Grey hulls. Norway to Canada, USA and East Africa. Cruising. **16** PENINSULAR AND ORIENTAL STEAM NAVIGATION CO., London. Various names for passenger liners. *Pando* — and *Strath*— for cargo liners. White/red, or black/red. UK to Far East. Cruising. Parent company of P & O Passenger Division, now the largest fleet of passenger ships in the world. Some purpose-built cruise liners (*Spirit of London*). **17** SWEDISH AMERICA LINE, Gothenburg. *—holm*. White/green or red. Sweden to USA and cruising. **18** GERMAN ATLANTIC LINE (Hanseatic Schiffahrts GmbH), Hamburg. Two ships: *Hanseatic* and *Hamburg*. White/red. Cruising. **19** CHANDRIS LINES, Piraeus, Greece. Names ending in *ia* or *is*. White or grey/red. Europe to America/Australia and New Zealand. Cruising. **20** POLISH OCEAN LINES (Polskie Linie Oceaniczne), Gdynia. Names of prominent Poles. Black or grey/red or green. Wide range of passenger and cargo services. **21** Union of Soviet Socialist Republics. State-owned passenger and cargo services, the latter with black funnels and red band. Some white hulls. Wide range of services.

Tankers (Plate 3)

Companies primarily concerned with the transportation of oil in bulk. Some other passenger and/or cargo companies owning tankers are indicated elsewhere. **1** ANDERS JAHRE, Sandefjord, Norway. *Ja*—. Grey/green. Also OBOs and cargo liners. **2** CHEVRON SHIPPING CO., STANDARD OIL and associated companies under flags of USA, the Netherlands, Liberia and Panama. Personal names and *Chevron* —. Black hulls. **3** NIARCHOS GROUP under flags of Greece, Liberia and Panama. Personal names and *World* —. Black/red. **4** HUNTING AND SON LTD, Newcastle-upon-Tyne. —*field*. Black/red. **5** ESSO PETROLEUM CO. LTD under flags of GB, USA, France, Belgium, Sweden, Denmark, West Germany and many other countries. *Esso* —. Second word name of town in relevant country. Black or grey/red. **6** NAESS GROUP under flags of GB, the Netherlands, France, Norway and Liberia. *Naess* —. Grey/green. **7** AP MÖLLER (Maersk Line), Copenhagen. — *Maersk*. Blue/red. **8** TEXACO INC. under flags of GB, USA, Norway, Liberia and Panama. *Texaco* —. Black/red, or white/green. **9** MOBIL OIL CORPORATION under flags of USA, France, West Germany, Liberia and Panama. Various names and *Mobil* —. Black or grey with white line/red. **10** TANKERS LTD (Athel Line Ltd), London. *Anco* — and *Athel*—. Black or grey/red. **11** BP TANKER CO. LTD, London. *British* —. Black/red. **12** TRIDENT TANKERS LTD (P & O Group), London. *Ard*— and —*a*. Black/red. **13** ONASSIS GROUP, Monrovia, Liberia. *Olympic* —. Black or white/red. **14** SHELL GROUP under flags of GB, France, the Nether-

lands, Liberia, Venezuela and Argentina. Names
of sea shells and *Shell* —. Black or grey/red.
15 BRITISH GOVERNMENT (Navy Department). Fleet oilers and small tankers. — *Rover*,
Ol—, *Tide*—, and —*leaf*. **16** SIG. BERGESEN
d.y. & CO., Oslo. *Berge* —. Light green hulls.
17 GULF OIL CORPORATION under flags
of USA, the Netherlands, Belgium and Liberia.
Gulf—, *Belgulf*— and other names. Blue-grey/
red. **18** LEIF HÖEGH & CO. A/S, Oslo.
Höegh—. Also dry cargo ships, car carriers,
ore/oil and LPG carriers. Grey/red. **19** SHELL-
MEX AND BP LTD, London. *Shell* —, *BP* —
(second word an occupation). Black/red. Distributors of oil and spirit by coastal and estuarine
tankers. **20** METCALFE MOTOR COASTERS
LTD, London. Personal names and *M*. Black
or grey/red. Distributors, coasting and home
trade. **21** ROWBOTHAM & SONS (MANAGE-
MENT) LTD, London. —*man*. Grey/blue.
Home trade.

**British Ocean-going Cargo Liners,
Container Ships and Bulk Carriers (1)
(Plate 4)**

1 SILVER LINE, London. *Silver* —. Black
or grey/red. **2** ANCHOR LINE LTD (Runciman Shipping Ltd), Glasgow. —*moor* and —*ia*.
UK to USA, Egypt, Pakistan and India. **3** STAG
LINE LTD (Joseph Robinson & Sons—Management Ltd), North Shields. Names of plants ending in *ia*. Black/red. Tramping. **4** THE
BOOTH STEAMSHIP CO. LTD, Liverpool.
Names of saints and artists. Black or grey/red.

Liverpool to South America; New York to West Indies: UK to Brazil and Peru. **5** MOSS HUTCHISON LINE LTD (P & O General Cargo Division), Liverpool. Middle East place names. Black/red. Some funnels as No. 34. UK to Mediterranean. **6** WM. FRANCE, FENWICK & CO. LTD, London. —*wood*. Black/red. Short-sea and ocean-going tramping. **7** BURIES MARKES LTD, London. *La* —. Black with white line/white. World-wide tramping. **8** HARRISON LINE (Thos. & James Harrison Ltd and The Charente Steamship Co. Ltd), Liverpool. Trades and professions. Black/pink. UK to Red Sea, South and East Africa, Central and South America. **9** BOWRING SS CO. LTD, (Seabridge Shipping Ltd associated with Bibby Bros), London. — *Bridge*. Grey/red. Bulk carriers. **10** SUGAR LINE LTD (Tate & Lyle Ltd), London. *Crystal* — and *Sugar* —. Black/red. Bulk cargoes, sugar. **11** HOULDER BROS & CO. LTD (Furness Withy Group), London. — *Grange* and —*bury*, and ore carriers *Or*—. Black or grey/red—some with white band. UK to South America and South Africa. Also tankers. **12** CLAN LINE STEAMERS LTD (British and Commonwealth Shipping Company), Glasgow. *Clan* — and *King* —. Black/pink. UK to South Africa, India, Ceylon and Bangladesh. BC burgee worn above house flag. **13** FURNESS WARREN LINE (Furness Withy Group), London. *Pacific* — and other names. Grey/green, or black/red. Liverpool to Canada and USA, Gulf ports and Pacific ports of North America. **14** PRINCE LINE LTD (Furness Withy Group), London. — *Prince*. Grey/red. UK to Mediterranean and various services. **15** T. & J. BROCKLEBANK LTD (Cunard Brocklebank Ltd), Liverpool.

Indian place names *M*—. Black with broad white line or white/red. UK to India, Ceylon and Pakistan. USA to same countries. **16** FRANK C. STRICK & CO. LTD (P & O General Cargo Division), London. —*istan*. Grey/red. Some funnels as No. 34. UK and Continent to Persian Gulf. **17** GLEN LINE LTD (Glen & Shire Line—Ocean Steam Ship Co. Ltd), Liverpool. *Glen*— and —*shire*. Black/pink. UK and Continent to Far East. **18** BIBBY BROTHERS & COMPANY, Liverpool. —*shire* and — *Bridge*. Black with yellow line/red. UK to Egypt, Ceylon and Far East. **19** PORT LINE LTD (Cunard Brocklebank Ltd), London. *Port* —. Grey/red. UK to Australia and New Zealand, and Canada to same countries. **20** CUNARD STEAM SHIP CO. LTD (Cunard Brocklebank Ltd), Liverpool. —*ia*. Black/red with white line. UK to USA, Gulf ports and Great Lakes. See No. 1 with regard to White Star flag. **21** SIR WILLIAM REARDON SMITH & SONS LTD, Cardiff. — *City*. Black/red. World-wide tramping.

British Ocean-going Cargo Liners, Container Ships and Bulk Carriers (2) (Plate 5)

22 FEDERAL STEAM NAVIGATION CO. LTD AND NEW ZEALAND S. CO. LTD (P & O General Cargo Division and joint company with the Danish J. Lauritzen Group), London. British counties. *Wild* — (names of birds) and N.w Zealand place names. Black/red, or light green/dark green. Reefers from Australia and

New Zealand to UK. North America to Australia and New Zealand. **23** BLUE STAR LINE LTD, London. — *Star*. Black/red, or blue grey/blue. UK to South America, South Africa, Australia and New Zealand, and West Indies. Also tankers, but mainly reefers. **24** MANCHESTER LINERS LTD (Furness Withy Group), Manchester. Red hulls with company name painted on hull. Container service from UK to USA, Canada and Great Lakes. **25** ELDER DEMPSTER LINES LTD (Ocean Steam Ship Company Ltd), Liverpool. African regions. Black/red, or white with yellow line/green. UK to West and South Africa; USA and Mediterranean to West Africa; India, East Pakistan to West Africa. **26** PACIFIC STEAM NAVIGATION COMPANY (Furness Withy Group), Liverpool. *Pacific* — and South American names. Black/green. UK to West Indies, Gulf ports, West and South America. **27** MacANDREWS & CO. LTD, London. Spanish names. White/green. UK to Spain and Morocco, Sicily and West Italy. **28** SCOTTISH SHIP MANAGEMENT LTD [Lyle Shipping Co. Ltd, H. Hogarth & Sons Ltd, and Lambert Bros (Shipping) Ltd], Glasgow. *Cape* —, *Baron* —. Grey/red. Bulk carriers, most vessels on long-term time charter. **29** BEN LINE STEAMERS LTD (Wm. Thomson & Co.). Leith. *Ben* — and *City of Edinburgh*. Grey/green. Container ships (flag with BLC instead of anchor) and conventional cargo liners. UK and Continent to the Far East. **30** BOWATER STEAM SHIP CO. LTD (Cayzer, Irvine & Co. Ltd), London. —*Bowater*. Dark green/light green. Newsprint and wood-pulp carriers from North America to Europe.

31 ATLANTIC CONTAINER LINE, Liverpool, Rotterdam, etc. *Atlantic C—* and *Atlantic S—*. Blue hulls. (Consortium of Cunard SS Co. Ltd, French Line, Holland America, Swedish America, two other Swedish companies, and one from West Germany.) **32** BANK LINE LTD (Andrew Weir & Co. Ltd), Glasgow or Belfast. *—bank*. Black/red. UK to South Seas, Australia and the Far East. East Africa to Far East; India to South America. Reefers. **33** FYFFES GROUP LTD, Glasgow. Some ships registered in Honduras and the Netherlands. West Indian names. Grey or white/red. UK to West Indies. Reefers. **34** PENINSULAR AND ORIENTAL STEAM NAVIGATION COMPANY (General Cargo Division and Bulk Shipping Division), London and other ports. *Pando—* and *Strath—*. Various names. Black hulls. In time this funnel will replace those given elsewhere for constituent companies. **35** ELLERMAN LINES LTD, London. *—ian, City of —*. Grey/red. Worldwide services under several companies in the group all with same funnel but different house flags. **36** THE GEEST LINE LTD, Boston (UK). *Geest—*. White/green. Europe to West Indies. Reefers specializing in carriage of bananas. **37** BLUE FUNNEL LINE (The Ocean Steam Ship Company Ltd), Liverpool. Names of Greek heroes. Black/pink, or white hull. General cargo and tankers. UK to Singapore, Thailand, Hong Kong and Japan. **38** LAMPORT & HOLT LINE LTD, Liverpool and London. Eminent men of letters, artists and musicians. Black with white band. UK to Brazil, River Plate and Paraguay. **39** HAINNOURSE LTD (P & O General Cargo Division), London. *Tre—*. Blue hulls. Some funnels as No. 34. General trading and tramping. Also tankers. **40** SIR R. ROPNER & CO. LTD,

Hartlepool. —*pool*. Green/light green. Tramping. **41** OVERSEAS CONTAINERS LTD (Consortium of B & C Shipping Group, Ocean Group, Furness Withy and P & O), London. — *Bay*. Green hulls. **42** PALM LINE LTD, London or Liverpool. — *Palm*. Grey/red. UK to West Africa.

Passenger and Car Ferries within the British Isles and to the Continent of Europe (Plate 6)

1 BRITISH RAIL, London. Various names. Dark blue or black/red—some with white line. SEALINK painted on ships' sides. Numerous passenger, cargo, car and train ferry services. **2** ISLE OF MAN STEAM PACKET CO. LTD, Douglas, Isle of Man. Manx names. Black/red with white line. Liverpool to Douglas; Belfast, Ardrossan, Fleetwood and Dublin to Douglas. Some summer services only. **3** ATLANTIC STEAM NAVIGATION CO. LTD, London. — *Ferry*. Black/red with white line. Preston to Larne and Belfast; other RO/RO and container services from Felixstowe to the Continent; Preston to Ireland. **4** TOWNSEND-THORESON LTD, Dover and Oslo. Townsend vessels: *Free Enterprise* —, with red funnel and green/red. Thoresen vessels: *Viking* —, with pale green funnels and orange/red. Dover to Calais and Zeebrugge; Southampton to Le Havre and Cherbourg. **5** ELLERMAN'S WILSON LINE LTD, Hull. —*o*. Green or grey/red. Hull to Zeebrugge. **6** BURNS & LAIRD LINES LTD (P & O Short Sea Shipping Sector), Glasgow. MV *Lion*. Black with white line/red. Ardrossan to Belfast. **7** CALEDONIAN MacBRAYNE

LTD (Scottish Transport Group), Glasgow.* *Loch* — and West of Scotland names. Numerous services in the Clyde estuary and the Inner and Outer Hebrides. **8 NORTH OF SCOTLAND ORKNEY AND SHETLAND SHIPPING CO. LTD** (P & O Short Sea Shipping Sector), Aberdeen. *St* — and *Earl of Zetland*. Black with white line/red. Aberdeen to Lerwick; Lerwick to northern isles of Shetland; Scrabster to Stromness. Also cargo services. RO/RO vessels on order. **9 BELFAST STEAMSHIP CO. LTD** (P & O Short Sea Shipping Sector), Belfast. Black with white line/red. Liverpool to Belfast. **10** P. & A. CAMPBELL LTD, Cardiff (owned by No. 4 above). Excursion vessels, Bristol Channel and South Coast. **11 SOUTHAMPTON, ISLE OF WIGHT & SOUTH OF ENGLAND ROYAL MAIL STEAM PACKET CO. LTD** (Red Funnel Line), Southampton. — *Castle*. Black/red. Southampton to Cowes, and excursions. **12** SOUTHERN FERRIES LTD (P & O Short Sea Shipping Sector), Southampton. MV *Eagle*. White with blue line/red. Southampton to Lisbon and Tangier. **13** NORMANDY FERRIES LTD (General Steam Navigation Co. Ltd— P & O Short Sea Shipping Sector and associated with S.A.G.A. Paris), Southampton. MV *Dragon* and MV *Leopard* (under French flag). White/red. Southampton to Le Havre. **14** BRITISH & IRISH STEAM PACKET CO. LTD, Dublin. Names of Irish counties and towns. Black/green, or blue/green. Liverpool–Dublin and Swansea–Cork. **15** THE UNITED STEAMSHIP CO. LTD (Det Forenede Dampskibs-Selskab A/S), Copenhagen. Various personal and place names including American states. Black or white/red.

* Livery not final at time of printing.

Harwich–Esbjerg.   Also Scandinavian and Mediterranean services.   **16** BERGEN LINE (Det Bergenske D/S), Bergen.   Mainly classic names. Black/red, or grey/green.   Newcastle–Stavanger and Bergen.   **17** SWEDISH LLOYD (Svenska Lloyd Rederi A/B), Gothenburg.   *—a.*   Grey or white/blue.   Southampton–Bilbao.   **18** NORTH SEA FERRIES (P & O Short Sea Shipping Sector), Hull.   *Nor—.*   Black with orange line/red. Hull–Rotterdam, Hull–Zeebrugge.   **19** FRED OLSEN LINE, Oslo.   *B—.*   Grey/green. Newcastle–Kristiansand   and   Oslo.   Harwich–Kristiansand.   Other services from Norway to Continent.   **20** TOR LINE, Stockholm.   *Tor —a.*   Blue hulls.   Immingham–Amsterdam. Immingham–Gothenburg.   Gothenburg–Amsterdam.   **21** PRINS FERRIES (Lion Ferry AB), Halmstad (Sweden).   *Prins —.*   White hulls. Harwich–Hamburg.   Harwich–Bremerhaven.

British Coaster and Home Trade Companies (Plate 7)

1 GEM LINE LTD (Wm. Robertson, Shipowners Ltd), Glasgow.   Names of gems.   Black/red.   **2** COAST LINES LTD (P & O Short Sea Shipping Sector), Liverpool.   — *Coast*, and breeds   of   dogs.   Black,   white   line/black. **3** GEORGE GIBSON & CO. LTD, Leith. Borders place names.   Black/red or red hull. **4** F. T. EVERARD & SONS LTD, London. — *Everard* or words referring to human qualities ending in *ity*, e.g. *Ability*.   **5** CURRIE LINE LTD (Walter Runciman & Co. Ltd), Leith. —*land*.   Associated with a German company, also CURRIE LINE painted on hull.   Black/red.

6 STEPHENSON CLARKE SHIPPING LTD, London and Newcastle. Place names of Sussex. Black with white line/red. **7** J. & A. GARDNER LTD, Glasgow. *Saint* —. Black with white line/green, or grey/green or black. **8** CORY MARITIME LTD, London. Mainly colliers. *Cor*—. Coastal tankers. *Pass of* —. Black/red. **9** JOHN STEWART & CO. (SHIPPING) LTD, Glasgow. *Yew*—. Black/red. **10** COMBEN LONGSTAFF & CO. LTD, London. —*brook*. Black/red. **11** LONDON & ROCHESTER TRADING CO. LTD (Crescent Line), Rochester. Various names, many ending in *ence*. Red brown with white or blue line/red. **12** JOHN KELLY LTD, Belfast. *Bally*—. Black/red. Colliers. **13** JAMES FISHER & SONS LTD, Barrow-in-Furness. — *Fisher*. Black with yellow line/red. Fleet includes two heavy lift ships. **14** UNITED BALTIC CORPORATION LTD, London. *Baltic* —. Grey or white/green. **15** HULL GATES SHIPPING CO. LTD (Boston Group Holdings Ltd), Hull. —*gate*. Blue-grey/green, or black with white line/red. Also coastal tankers. **16** THOMAS WATSON (SHIPPING) LTD, Rochester. *Lady* —. Blue/red. **17** S. W. COE & CO. LTD, Liverpool. —*thorn*. Grey or black/red. **18** HUDSON STEAMSHIP CO. LTD, London. *Hudson* —. Black/red. **19** CENTRAL ELECTRICITY GENERATING BOARD, London. Personal names and London place names. Black with white topline/red. **20** J. R. RIX & SONS LTD, Hull. —*rix*. Green with white topline/red. **21** KLONDYKE SHIPPING CO. LTD, Hull. —*dyke*. Grey or black/red.

5 WARSHIPS

General Characteristics

Colour In all countries naval vessels are painted grey. Ships of the Royal Navy are painted light grey, with white topmasts if they are in commission; in reserve, the topmasts are painted grey. On service in certain eastern waters the ships are painted white. All British submarines are painted black. **General appearance** The warship's long, low outline is broken by gun houses and controls, with the main superstructure building up near or around the foremast. This mast, and the mainmast or tower, has a large number of radar antennae and aerials, and unlike the cargo ship the warship never has a raised poop. She is generally flush decked and may have a long forecastle deck which extends well aft. Some frigates have a raised forecastle, but this is quite distinct

---

Fig. 109 Parts of a Warship. British 'County' class guided missile destroyer. **a** and **b** 115-mm-radar-controlled fully automatic dual-purpose quick-firing guns in twin turrets. **f** forecastle. **js** jackstaff. **n** navigating bridge. **gr** gun control radar. **sr** search radar. **sh** signal halyards. **t** topmast. **awr** air warning search radar. **l** launches and inflatable rafts. **sc** close-range anti-aircraft missile launcher. **mr** missile guidance radar. **h** helicopter landing deck. **ss** medium-range guided missile launcher. **q** quarter deck. **es** ensign staff. **D** pennant number for destroyers

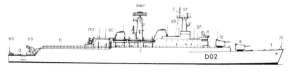

from that of a cargo liner. **Propulsion** Most fighting ships are propelled by high pressure steam turbines and oil-fired water-tube boilers. Although now common for merchant ships, diesel engines are much less used for warships. Some frigates, most minesweepers and patrol vessels do have motor engines, and the latter can be combined with gas turbines—CODOG propulsion. Gas turbines have been introduced in several classes of vessel in various combinations. COGOG indicates that a ship has two sets of gas turbines—one for full power and the other for cruising. COSAG combines geared steam turbines and gas turbines. Nuclear-powered steam turbine vessels have been in operation for some years. In the Royal Navy this method is confined to ballistic missile and fleet submarines, but in the United States Navy some aircraft carriers, missile cruisers and missile frigates are propelled in this way, as well as ballistic missile and attack submarines. **Protection** The now obsolete battleship was protected amidships by armour plating up to 400 mm in thickness, but the average armour used on present-day ships is very much thinner. Cruisers are built with some protection at water-line and round certain vital parts of the ship, but destroyers, frigates and other warships have no additional protection at all. **Subdivision of the hull** Another difference between the structure of a cargo vessel and that of a fighting ship is that the former hull is divided into six or eight large compartments by watertight transverse bulkheads. On the other hand the warship, with no large cargo holds, is divided by many transverse and longitudinal watertight bulkheads into a great number of small compartments; these can be sealed off by watertight doors if there has been flooding by accident or naval action.

Calibre	Mounting, and other characteristics	Type of warship
Guns 6 in. (152 mm)	Twin mounting in armoured turrets, fully automatic. Dual purpose, high and low angle. 20 rounds per minute	Cruisers. Triple mounting
4·5 in (115 mm)	Single or twin mountings in armoured turrets; fully automatic radar-controlled. Dual purpose	Guided missile destroyers, frigates
4 in. (102 mm)	Single or twin mountings in lightly armoured gunhouses	Anti-submarine frigates—older types
3 in. (76 mm)	Twin mounting in armoured turrets. 90 rounds per minute	Cruisers
40 mm	Bofors guns. Mounting of one, two or six barrels. Open or light shields. High speed close range anti-aircraft guns. May be fully automatic and radar-controlled.	Standard AA guns for all fighting ships and some auxiliaries
20 mm	Oerlikon—single mounting. Heavy machine guns	Secondary armament of small warships such as mine-sweepers
Guided Missiles Polaris 9·45 m*	Inter-continental ballistic missiles; range up to 2,500 miles	Resolution class submarines
Exocet 5·12 m	All weather surface-to-surface missile (French)	'County' class guided missile destroyers
Seadart	Medium-range surface-to-air missile, twin launcher	Destroyers
Seaslug 5·995 m*	Long-range anti-aircraft missile, twin launchers	'County' class guided missile armed destroyers
Seacat 1·48 m*	Short-range anti-aircraft missile, quadruple or twin launchers. To be replaced by Seawolf	Destroyers, frigates, carriers and increasing number of types. Fast patrol boats
Torpedoes Ikara 3·35 m*	Long-range anti-submarine homing torpedo	'Type 82' armed destroyers
21 in (533 mm)	Single, triple, quadruple or pentad swivelling or fixed mounts	Resolution and Valiant class submarines, patrol submarines, some frigates, MTBs
Depth-charge Mortars i.e. anti-submarine mortar bombs		
Squib	Triple-barrelled mountings, short range	Destroyers, frigates
Limbo	Long barrel triple launchers. Automatic depth setting from ASDIC	Anti-submarine frigates

* Length of missile

Fig. 110 Comparative silhouettes of British
Warships and Auxiliaries (1)

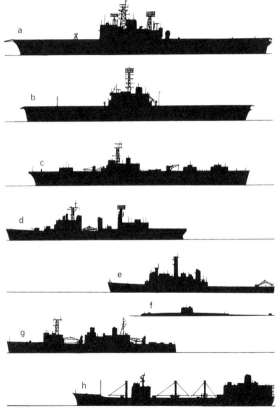

Type and/or class (number of class in 1973)	Date* and refit	Tonnes†	o.a. (metres)	Page ref.
a Aircraft carrier HMS *Ark Royal* (1)	1955 (1970)	43,060	257·6	123
b Commando Ship (2)	1954 (1962)	23,300	224·9	123
c Depot ship HMS *Triumph*	1946 (1965)	13,500	213·1	152
d Helicopter Cruiser (2) HMS *Blake*	1961 (1968)	9,500	172·8	133
e Assault ship HMS *Fearless* (2)	1965	11,060	158·5	135
f Nuclear Ballistic Missile Submarine HMS *Resolution* (4)	1967	7,500 (8,400)	129·5	147
g Submarine Depot Ship HMS *Defiance* (1) (ex-HMS *Forth*)	1939 (1966)	10,000 (gt)	161·8	152
h Replenishment ship RFA *Regent*	1965	18,029	195·1	161

* First of the class
† Standard displacement (referred to as *tonnes* weight to distinguish from *tons* capacity)

Fig. 111 'County' class guided missile destroyer firing a surface-to-air missile

Fig. 112   Comparative silhouettes of British Warships and Auxiliaries (2)

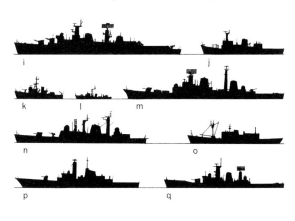

Type, name or class (number of class in 1.73)	Date (and refit)	Tonnes	o.a. (metres)	Page ref.
i Guided Missile Destroyer 'County' class (9)	1962	5,200	158·7	113
j Survey Ship HMS *Hecla* (3)	1965	2,898 gt	79·3	155
k Coastal minesweeper 'Ton' class (38)	1953	360	46·6	151
l Seaward Defence Boat 'Ford' class (2)	1956	120	35·6	—
m Guided Missile Destroyer HMS *Bristol* (1)	1972	5,650	154·5	139
n Guided Missile Destroyer HMS *Sheffield* (1)	1973	3,500	125·0	139
o Ice Patrol Ship HMS *Endurance* (1)	1956 (1968)	3,600	91·4	—
p General Purpose Frigate ('Type 21') HMS *Amazon* (1)	1973	2,500	117·0	143
q General Purpose Frigate HMS *Leander* (26)	1963	2,450	113·4	143
r AS Frigate HMS *Rothesay* (12) (with *Whitby* class)	1960	2,380	112·8	141, 143
s GP Frigate 'Tribal' class (7)	1961	2,300	109·7	143
t AA Frigate HMS *Leopard* (4)	1957	2,300	103·6	143
u Fast Patrol Boat HMS *Scimitar* (3)	1969	—	30·4	—

118

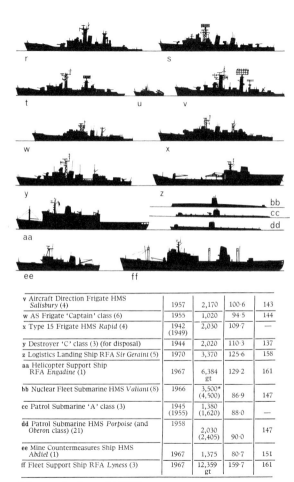

r			
s			
t	u	v	
w	x		
y	z		
aa	bb	cc	dd
ee	ff		

v Aircraft Direction Frigate HMS *Salisbury* (4)	1957	2,170	100·6	143
w AS Frigate 'Captain' class (6)	1955	1,020	94·5	144
x Type 15 Frigate HMS *Rapid* (4)	1942 (1949)	2,030	109·7	—
y Destroyer 'C' class (3) (for disposal)	1944	2,020	110·3	137
z Logistics Landing Ship RFA *Sir Geraint* (5)	1970	3,370	125·6	158
aa Helicopter Support Ship RFA *Engadine* (1)	1967	6,384	129·2	161
bb Nuclear Fleet Submarine HMS *Valiant* (8)	1966	3,500* (4,500)	86·9	147
cc Patrol Submarine 'A' class (3)	1945 (1955)	1,380 (1,620)	88·0	—
dd Patrol Submarine HMS *Porpoise* (and *Oberon* class) (21)	1958	2,030 (2,405)	90·0	147
ee Mine Countermeasures Ship HMS *Abdiel* (1)	1967	1,375	80·7	151
ff Fleet Support Ship RFA *Lyness* (3)	1967	12,359 gt	159·7	161

* tonnage-surface (tonnage-submerged)

Fig. 113   Guided Missile Destroyer HMS *Bristol*

Pennant Letters of British Warships

R Aircraft carriers or commando carriers. **S** Submarines. **L** Assault ships, logistic landing ships and landing craft. **C** Cruisers. **D** Destroyers. **F** Frigates. **N** Minelayers. **K** Helicopter support ships. **M** Minesweepers—coastal and inshore. **P** Seaward defence boats, boom defence vessels, coastal patrol and fast patrol vessels. **A** Support ships and auxiliaries.

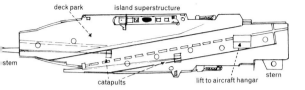

deck park   island superstructure

stem

catapults

lift to aircraft hangar   stern

Fig. 114 Angled flight deck of
a fixed wing aircraft carrier

Aircraft Carrier

The aircraft carrier is easily recognized by her
size and the immense, clear deck with neither
camber nor sheer, which stretches the full length
and width of the ship.   The funnel, control tower
and navigating bridge form a narrow island superstructure on the starboard side.   The search and
aircraft direction radars, and other aerials on either
lattice masts or towers are also situated on the
superstructure.   The carrier has no offensive
weapons but is equipped with a few 115-mm and/
or quadruple surface-to-air missile launchers.
The service speed of the bigger carriers is between
30 and 35 knots; in all cases the ships are propelled
by geared turbines.   The flight deck, hangars and
machinery spaces are protected by armour plating
up to 100 mm in thickness, and round the hull, at
the water-line, is a belt of armour slightly more
than that in thickness.   The flight deck of a fixed
wing aircraft carrier is now always set at an angle
of about 8° from the centre line.   This British in-
vention increases the efficiency of the aircraft on
landing, and gives parking space forward of the
superstructure.   Aircraft are assisted in take-off
by steam catapults—a system also invented by the
British.   Aircraft are normally stowed in hangars
below the flight deck with access by either centre-
line or side lifts.

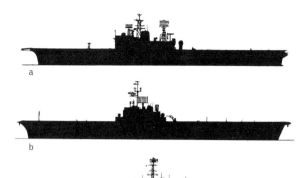

a

b

c

Fig. 115 Aircraft carriers

Aircraft carriers

a HMS *Ark Royal* 1955 (refitted 1970)/43,060 tonnes/257·6 m overall length/Steam turbines with quadruple screws/31·5 knots. This British vessel now carries 30 fixed wing aircraft and six helicopters. She has a large crew of 2,640 officers and men when she is acting as flagship, and rather fewer on ordinary duties. HMS *Ark Royal* is the last of the traditional fleet aircraft carriers as her slightly smaller partner has been withdrawn from service preparatory to disposal. **b** French *Clemenceau* (and *Foch*) 1961/27,307 tonnes/265 m/Steam turbines and twin screws/24 knots service speed. With a capacity for 40 aircraft, this vessel has a defensive armament of eight 100-mm automatic guns in single turrets. **c** Commando ship 23,300 tonnes/224·9 m/Steam turbines and twin screws/28 knots. During the last war a number of light carriers of about 14,000 tonnes displacement were built and some of these are still in use in the navies of Australia, India, Argentina, France and Brazil. A number of the ships were laid down during the war but not completed until several years afterwards. The drawing **c** represents a number of larger ships laid down or launched about the same time, and now converted to commando carriers with facilities for carrying 20 helicopters, landing-craft, motor vehicles and other equipment necessary for a shore operation. The vehicles can be carried ashore by helicopters. The commando carrier has no need for an angled deck or steam catapults, but the profile does not differ in general from that of the fixed wing carrier.

Official US Navy photograph

Fig. 116 Nuclear-powered attack carrier USS *Enterprise* 1961/75,700 tonnes/341·3 m/35 k. The first nuclear-powered warship and the largest warship ever built, but will be surpassed by the three *Nimitz* class carriers. She carries about 100 fixed wing aircraft and has four steam catapults and four lifts giving access to the hangars. The nuclear reactor unit for providing steam to the turbines requires no funnel uptakes, therefore the superstructure is small and less vulnerable to air attack. For defence she is equipped with short-range supersonic anti-aircraft missiles.

Fig. 117 The 20-metre overhang of the flight deck and side lift of USS *Forrestal* 1955/60,000 tonnes/80 aircraft

124

Cruiser

Until the period shortly after the Second World War, the term *cruiser* was used to define a clearly understood type of fighting ship divided into two categories: *heavy* cruisers with a main armament of eight-inch (203-mm) guns and *light* cruisers equipped with six-inch (152-mm) guns. Although it was gun power rather than size which determined the category, the heavy cruiser was usually in the 10/14,000 tonnes range, while the light cruiser was often as small as 4,500 tonnes displacement.

The duties of the cruiser were many: she had to protect seaborne trade routes by escorting convoys, search for and attack commerce raiders, give protection from aircraft and submarines, and form part of a defensive screen for larger warships such as aircraft carriers and battleships. For these duties she had to be equipped with a diversity of weapons; she had to be fast, and she had to be designed for spending long periods at sea without refuelling. Some of the wartime United States heavy cruisers remain converted to missile cruisers, and a small number retain their original gun armament as potential Fire Support Ships in reserve. Of other nations only Spain keeps the 1936 heavy cruiser *Canarias*, a British-built version of the 'County' class cruisers of which HMS *Norfolk* was a well-known example. Many light cruisers have similarly been converted, partially or wholly, for the use of guided missiles: surface-to-air guided missiles and new anti-submarine weapons that replace the traditional guns. The term cruiser now refers to the largest combatant naval unit, after the aircraft carrier, and one which is a powerfully armed, fast ship able to search out and destroy enemy aircraft, surface and underwater craft.

Guided Missile Cruiser

The guided missile cruiser may be either a converted gun cruiser or a purpose-built vessel. Some cruisers retain a small number of conventional guns, but the main armament consists of surface-to-air and AS missile launchers. The largest ship in this category is the USS *Long Beach* (**Fig. 121**), a nuclear-powered ship of 14,200 tonnes standard displacement, built in 1961. Her armament consists of three twin surface-to-air launchers, an eight tube AS launcher, two triple tube torpedo units and two single 127-mm dual-purpose AA guns. **a** United States *Albany* class 1940s 13,700 tonnes/205·3 m/ST/33 k converted in the 1960s from orthodox heavy cruisers armed with 203-mm (8-in) guns. The very tall funnels and high control tower are quite distinctive. Armament consists of four surface-to-air launchers, two triple torpedo tubes and two 127-mm guns. **b** United States *California* class 1973/ 10,000 tonnes/181·7 m/Nuclear power ST/30 knots. Officially referred to as a frigate in USA nomenclature, it is in all respects, i.e. armament, speed and size, similar to the guided missile cruiser of other nations. **c** Russian *Kresta II* class 1970/6,000 tonnes/158 m/ST/33 k. Armament consists of surface-to-surface and surface-to-air launchers, AS weapons and ten torpedo tubes. The superstructure amidships is even more festooned with radar scanners and aerials than the normal up-to-date warship. Aft of the after missile launcher is a helideck and hangar for a single helicopter. **d** Netherlands *De Zeven Provincien* class 1953/9,529 tonnes/188·7 m/ST/32 k. Built as an all-gun cruiser she has been converted to a guided missile cruiser with a mixed armament and a strong bias towards conventional gunnery. She has a twin missile launcher aft, but four twin turret 152-mm guns and a large number of 57-mm and 40-mm AA guns.

Fig. 118 Guided missile cruisers

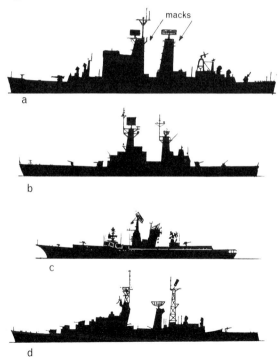

a

b

c

d

Fig. 119 French cruiser *Colbert* with conventional guns forward and guided missile launchers aft

Fig. 120 Guided missile cruiser USS *Springfield*

Fig. 121

Nuclear-powered cruiser USS *Long Beach*

Cruisers

Five ex-Royal Navy cruisers are still in operation after having been sold to other navies. The Indian Navy purchased two of these ships; **a** *Delhi* was a *Leander* class light cruiser of 7,000 tonnes, built in 1933 and refitted in 1955. She is still armed with six 152-mm guns, eight 102-mm and fourteen 40-mm AA guns. As HMS *Achilles*, she was famous for the part she played in the Battle of the River Plate in the winter of 1939 when, with the cruisers HMS *Ajax* and HMS *Exeter*, she helped to defeat the German pocket battleship *Graf Spee*. India also has the *Mysore*, ex-HMS *Nigeria*, built in 1940 as a 'Colony' class light cruiser. **b** The Pakistan Navy purchased the *Dido* class anti-aircraft light cruiser HMS *Diadem* and renamed her *Babur*/1944/5,900 tonnes/156·1 m/ ST/32 k. The Peruvian navy has two ex-*Ceylon* class light cruisers *Almirante Grau* (ex-HMS *Newfoundland*) and *Coronel Bolognesi* (ex-HMS *Ceylon*) shown in silhouette **c**.

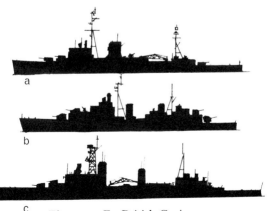

Fig. 122 Ex-British Cruisers

A good example of a British all-gun light cruiser has now been preserved as a permanent exhibit. HMS *Belfast* is berthed in the Thames, opposite the Tower of London, and is open to the public. As the largest cruiser of the Second World War, she was completed by Harland and Wolff in 1939 with a full load displacement of 14,930 tonnes. Her armament consists of twelve six-inch (152-mm) guns in triple turrets, and a number of 40-mm AA guns. When she was refitted in 1959 her torpedo tubes were removed and the tripod masts were replaced by lattice structures. The cruiser will be remembered for the important part she played in the Battle of North Cape, in December 1943, when the German battleship *Scharnhorst* was destroyed while attempting to intercept a Russia-bound Allied convoy. In the action with HMS *Belfast* were the battleship HMS *Duke of York*, the heavy cruiser HMS *Norfolk*, two light cruisers, HMS *Sheffield* and *Jamaica*, and eight destroyers.

Fig. 123 HMS *Belfast* at her permanent berth near Tower Bridge

P. A. Vicary

Fig. 124 Helicopter cruiser HMS *Blake* converted from conventional all-gun cruiser

Crown copyright

Fig. 125

French helicopter cruiser *Jeanne d'Arc*

By courtesy of French Naval Attaché

Fig. 126 Italian helicopter cruiser *Vittorio Veneto*

By courtesy of Italian Naval Attaché

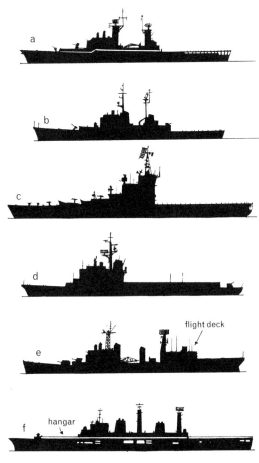

Fig. 127 Helicopter cruisers

Helicopter Cruisers

Although many warships of different types are now equipped with a helicopter-landing platform, the helicopter cruiser is quite distinctive. The high flight deck is an unobstructed area extending to between one-third and one-half of the full length of the vessel.

Fig. 127 a Italian *Vittorio Veneto* 1969/7,500 tonnes 170 m/ST/32 k. Designed as a multi-purpose ship, she carries a squadron of nine helicopters and is armed with a twin surface-to-air missile launcher forward, eight 76-mm guns and torpedo tubes. **b** Italian *Andrea Doria* class guided missile escort cruiser 1964/5,000 tonnes/ 149·3 m/30 k is a smaller version of **a** with a similar armament but much smaller flight deck. **c** Russian *Moskva* class helicopter missile cruiser 1967/15,000 tonnes/196·6 m/ST/30 k. Very unconventional in appearance, this vessel can carry up to 30 helicopters and is armed with surface-to-air and anti-submarine missiles and torpedo tubes. The enormous funnel forms the mainmast and major part of the bridge superstructure. **d** French *Jeanne d'Arc* 1964/10,000 tonnes/182 m/ST/26·5 k eight helicopters and armed with four 100-mm guns two of which are placed at the stern. **e** HMS *Blake* 1961/9,500 tonnes/172·8 m/ST/31 k. One of three ships designed and built as general purpose all-gun cruisers of the traditional type. Two have now been converted to helicopter cruisers retaining only one twin mount of 152-mm fully automatic guns. In addition they are armed with 76-mm AA guns. **f** Projected British through-deck helicopter cruiser to have an angled flight deck almost the full length of the vessel, for helicopters and other aircraft. She will be propelled by gas turbines.

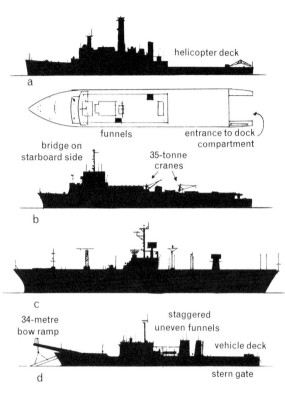

helicopter deck

a

funnels   entrance to dock
                           compartment

bridge on
starboard side   35-tonne
                      cranes

b

c

34-metre   staggered
bow ramp   uneven funnels

                  vehicle deck

d   stern gate

Fig. 128 Assault landing ships

Assault Landing Ships

a HMS *Fearless* and *Intrepid* 1965–7/11,060 tonnes/158·5 m/ST/21 k. With a full load this type of ship can carry four landing craft on davits, four landing craft (mechanized) in the dock, fifteen tanks and a number of heavy vehicles on the helicopter deck. There is accommodation for 350 troops, as well as a crew of over 500, including military engineers, and communications units. As multi-purpose ships they can serve as naval and brigade headquarters in a seaborne assault operation, carry assault troops and their armour, and offer maintenance facilities for other vessels. **b** French *Orage* 1968/5,800 tonnes/149 m/M/17 k. This assault ship and her sister, fulfil the same purpose as **a** and have similar facilities for carrying landing craft, tanks and troops. An unusual feature is the narrow bridge placed on the starboard side as on aircraft carriers. **c** USS *Blue Ridge* 1970/19,290 tonnes full load/188·5 m/ST/ 20 k. This amphibious command ship, with the high freeboard and continuous deck, resembles an aircraft carrier. Her duty is to act as command and control centre in an assault which involves sea, land, air and amphibious forces. Conspicuous are the numerous radar towers and aerials. **d** USS *Newport* 1969/8,342 tonnes full load/158·7 m/M/20 k. One of a large series of tank landing craft with a higher speed than earlier types. Instead of a hinged bow door forward, similar to those used in craft of the last war, a bow ramp is hinged at deck level and operated by derricks which project over the stem. At the stern, a gate allows vehicles to pass from the tank direct to water level. Like **a**, the two funnels are *en echelon*, but in this case they are also different in width.

Fig. 129
French guided
missile destroy
Duquesne

*By courtesy of
French Naval
Attaché*

Fig. 130 Swedish destroyer *Östergötland* with
mixed armament of conventional guns and guided
missile launchers   *By courtesy of Swedish Naval Attaché*

Fig. 131 Nuclear-powered guided missile frigate
USS *Truxton*   *Official US Navy photogr*

Destroyers

In the 1890s the need arose for a fast, well-armed and seaworthy vessel to counteract the torpedo-boat, and the shipbuilding firm of Yarrow designed such a boat which proved a great success. Known as a *torpedo-boat destroyer* her functions gradually broadened, and eventually the term was simplified to *destroyer*, as she became an important multi-purpose unit in every fleet. Size, speed and armament increased, and during the Second World War many destroyers reached the 2,000-tonne mark with guns of light cruiser calibre.

The term destroyer persists but now it has no particular meaning; it is usually given to a class of fighting ship smaller, but much faster, than a cruiser with a mixed armament of all, or some, of the following weapons: orthodox guns, surface-to-air and surface-to-surface guided missiles, AS homing missiles, conventional torpedoes and depth-charge mortars. As before, the destroyer's duties are many, and she may be employed as an escort giving powerful AA and AS protection, take part in surface action with similar forces, or give support to landing operations. The British 'County' class guided missile armed destroyers are designed so that in the event of contamination by radio-active material they can be completely washed down. All-gun destroyers are still numerous, although many are gradually refitted with at least one guided missile launcher. Many ex-British *Daring*, 'Battle' and 'C' class destroyers still operate in Commonwealth and other navies. The United States Navy—their large destroyers are known as frigates—retain about 150 destroyers built during the last war; many of these have been refitted, with new electronic equipment.

Fig. 132 Guided missile destroyers

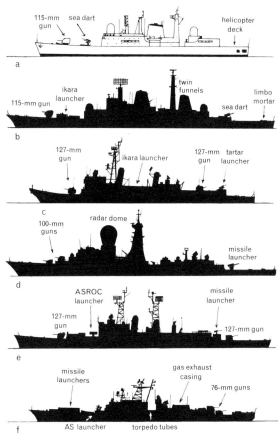

a — 115-mm gun, sea dart, helicopter deck

b — 115-mm gun, ikara launcher, twin funnels, sea dart, limbo mortar

c — 127-mm gun, ikara launcher, 127-mm gun, tartar launcher

d — 100-mm guns, radar dome, missile launcher

e — ASROC launcher, 127-mm gun, missile launcher, 127-mm gun

f — missile launchers, gas exhaust casing, 76-mm guns, AS launcher, torpedo tubes

Guided Missile Destroyers

A drawing of the Royal Navy 'County' class guided missile armed destroyer is shown on page 113. **Fig. 132 a** HMS *Sheffield* 1972/3,500 tonnes full load/125 m/COGOG/30 k. The first of the 'Type 42' class gas turbine ships—one set for full power and one for cruising. Armed with one 115-mm gun, twin 'Sea Dart' surface-to-air missile launcher, two 20-mm AA guns, AS torpedoes launched by helicopter. **b** HMS *Bristol* 1972/5,650 tonnes/154·5 m/COSAG/30 k. 'Type 82' propelled by combined steam and gas turbines. One 115-mm gun, one 'Sea Dart' missile launcher, 'Ikara' AS missile launcher, one 'Limbo' depth-charge mortar. Unusual with three funnels. **c** Royal Australian Navy *Brisbane* 1968/3,370 tonnes/132·2 m/ST/35 k. Armed with 'Tartar' surface-to-air and 'Ikara' anti-submarine missile launchers, two 127-mm guns, two triple torpedo tubes. Built in the USA and similar in design to US destroyers. **d** French guided missile leader *Duquesne* 1969/5,090 tonnes/157·6 m/ST/34 k. Easily distinguished by the radome. Armed with surface-to-air missile launchers and AS homing torpedo launcher and tubes. **e** *Mitscher* class 1953/1968/5,155 tonnes full load/150·3 m/ST/35 k. Armed with two 127-mm guns, a surface-to-air missile launcher and an eight tube AS ASROC torpedo launcher. The large class of *Charles F. Adams* class destroyers, built in the 1960s, are similarly armed. **f** Russian *Krivak* class 1971/3,540 tonnes/130m/GT/33 k. Armed with surface-to-air and AS rocket launchers, eight conventional torpedo tubes and four 76-mm guns. One distinguishing feature is the squat gas exhaust casing which does not resemble any other type of ship's funnel.

Frigates

In the early nineteenth century a frigate was described as 'a light nimble ship built for the purpose of sailing swiftly'. The term however went out of use until after the last war, when it was found that the corvette was too small and the conventional destroyer had ceased to serve its original purpose. As a result, destroyers became specialist AA or AS ships and smaller, lighter versions with similar functions were developed and known as frigates. Since then the specialist frigates have given way to more general purpose ships. In the Royal Navy, and many other navies, the frigate is primarily intended for fast escort duties and is equipped with AA and AS armament, and long-range detection gear. In the US Navy, however, the term frigate is applied to a ship above 5,000 tonnes with armament more akin to that of the light cruiser. The nuclear-powered guided missile frigates USS *Bainbridge* and *California* class are examples. The French 5,090-tonne ships of the *Suffren* class are known as *frégates lance-engins*, and many of the same country's frigate-type ships are known as escorts.

The modern frigate is then a fast ship with a mixed armament of guns, missiles and torpedoes, designed to outpace nuclear submarines and to do many duties in connection with fleet and convoy escort. In 1968 HMS *Exmouth*, built in 1957 as an anti-submarine frigate, was converted to gas turbine power and became the first warship to be thus propelled. Since then new British destroyers and frigates have been designed with the COGOG system of propulsion, i.e. complete gas turbines as compared with the ships of some foreign navies building CODOG—combined diesel and gas turbine-propulsion.

Fig. 133 British *Leander* class general purpose frigate

Crown copyright

Fig. 134
British
Whitby class
AS frigate
showing twin
113-mm
gun turret
and detail of
the bridge
and mast

Fig. 135
Further
detail
of the
same frigate
showing
the two
Limbo three-
barrelled
depth-charge
mortars

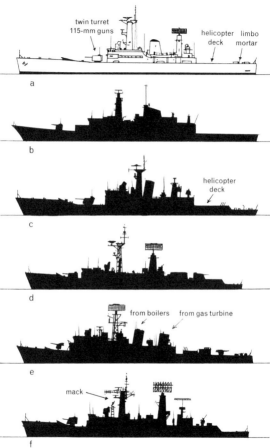

Fig. 136 British frigates

British Frigates

a General Purpose Frigate *Leander* class 1963–72/ 2,450+ tonnes/113·4 m/ST/30 k. Twenty-six ships in the RN. Armed with two 115-mm guns in a twin turret, two 40-mm, two 20-mm AA guns, 'Seacat' AA missile launcher, 'Limbo' depth-charge mortar, and a helicopter capable of delivering homing torpedoes. **b** Type 21 *Amazon* class 1973–1974/2,500 tonnes full load/117 m/COGOG/ 30+ k. Full gas turbine-propelled fast frigate. Armed with 'Seacat' or 'Seawolf' AA missile launchers, one 115-mm gun, two 20-mm AA, AS homing torpedoes from helicopter, six torpedo tubes. Controllable pitch propellors. **c** AS frigate *Rothesay* class. 1960–1/2,280 tonnes/112·8 m/ST/30 k. Armament similar to *Leander* class. Easily identified by funnel very close to mast. **d** AA frigate *Leopard* class. 1957–9/2,300 tonnes/ M 103·6 m/M/24 k. Armed with two twin turrets with 115-mm guns, one 40-mm or 'Seacat' launcher, one Squid AS mortar. Main function to protect convoys. Funnel within lattice mast. **e** General purpose frigate 'Tribal' class 1961–4/ 2,300 tonnes/109·7 m/COSAG/28 k. The only British two-funnel frigates. Designed as escort with strong AA and AS protection. Steam turbines provide main power and gas turbine as booster or to start from cold in an emergency. **f** Aircraft Direction Frigate *Salisbury* class 1957– 1960/2,170 tonnes/100·6 m/M/24 k. Identified by two 'macks', i.e. combined funnels and radar masts. Armed with two 115-mm guns in twin turret forward, Seacat missile launcher, or 40-mm AA guns, Squid depth-charge mortar. Main function is to direct shore or carrier-based aircraft and to act as destroyer in surface action.

Light Escort Vessels

It is difficult to make a clear distinction between a destroyer and a frigate and, similarly, the dividing line between the frigate and the escort is not always clear. Many frigates have a displacement tonnage of around 2,000, but the light escort vessel is generally about half that figure. During the Second World War the corvette—based on the very seaworthy whale catcher—fulfilled the function of a light convoy escort and patrol vessel. The Royal Navy's *Blackwood* ('Captain') class 2nd-rate frigates, with a tonnage of just over 1,000 tons, are lightly armed and have similar characteristics to the light escort vessel; some of them have been used for Fishery Protection. The Icelandic Coast Guard Patrol vessels such as the *Aegir* are lightly armed 1,000-tonne corvette-type ships designed for fishery protection.

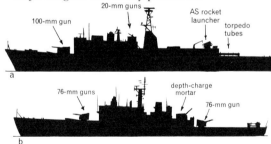

Fig. 137 a French Escort Vessel (Aviso) 1970s/ 950 tonnes/80 m/M/24 k. Armed with one 100-mm and two 20-mm AA guns and depth-charge and torpedo AS throwers. **b** Italian *de Cristofaro* class corvette 1966/850 tonnes/80·2 m/ 18 k. Armed with two 76-mm guns and AS armament similar to **a**.

Submarines

The essential character of the submarine's appearance is the long, narrow hull, and the single compact superstructure. The nuclear-powered submarine has a streamlined, whale-shaped hull with a blunt nose, and the bridge is placed much further forward than on the traditional vessel. Some conventionally powered submarines have additional domelike structures on deck which house the Sonar underwater detection gear. US nuclear-powered submarines have diving planes placed horizontally on each side of the bridge—known as the sail. Conventional propulsion is by diesels, for operating at surface and periscope level, and for charging batteries ready for deep operation on electric propulsion.

Since the Second World War the submarine has developed into a formidable strategic weapon of devastating power and world-wide range. The *snort* (first used by the Germans during the war) is a breathing tube, or air mast, which projects above the bridge and enables the vessel to take in fresh air while cruising just below the surface, and to remain submerged for much longer periods. The introduction of nuclear power has meant that the vessels are true submarines—and not just submersible vessels—able to cruise for thousands of miles without refuelling and without surfacing. Continuous fresh air is obtained by circulation through a regenerative plant. The *Polaris* and later *Poseidon* type guided missiles, with nuclear warheads, can be launched from a submarine when she is submerged and can be directed to targets over 2,000 miles away. The function of the Polaris guided missile submarine is to deliver the missiles on distant land targets, but she can operate in true naval actions, and for this purpose is equipped with standard 533-mm torpedoes.

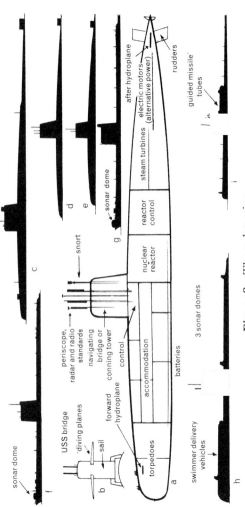

Fig. 138 The submarine

sonar dome

USS bridge
diving planes
sail
forward
hydroplane

periscope,
radar and radio
standards
navigating
bridge or
conning tower
control

snort

sonar dome

torpedoes

accommodation

batteries

3 sonar domes

swimmer delivery
vehicles

nuclear
reactor

reactor
control

steam turbines

after hydroplane

electric motors
(alternative power)

rudders

guided missile
tubes

a   b   c   d   e   f   g   h   i

Submarines in the world's navies fall into three main categories; these can be represented by examples from the Royal Navy. **c** Nuclear-powered Ballistic Missile Submarine *Resolution* class, 1967-9/7,500 tonnes surface—8,400 tonnes submerged/129·5 m/NST/20 k surface and 25 k submerged. Armed with Polaris surface-to-surface intercontinental missiles. Also six 533-mm torpedo homing tubes forward. Each submarine has two separate crews of 141 each in order to allow the greatest possible time at sea on very long operations. **d** Nuclear-powered Fleet Submarine *Valiant* class 1966 onwards/3,500 tonnes surface and 4,500 tonnes submerged/86·9 m and 82·9 m/NST/30 k. These ships are designed as true warships to hunt and kill enemy submarines and surface ships, and are equipped with six 533-mm torpedo tubes. Drawing **e** shows the profile of the slightly smaller prototype HMS *Dreadnought*. Like other nuclear-powered submarines her underwater efficiency is assisted by the whale-shaped hull and streamlined bridge. **f** Patrol Submarine *Oberon* class 1960-7/2,030 tonnes surface and 2,410 tonnes submerged/90·0 m/M and E/12 k surface and 17 submerged. Armed with eight tubes for standard 533-mm homing torpedoes. Part of the superstructure is made of glass fibre laminate. **g** *Porpoise* class 1958-61/2,030 tonnes surface and 2,405 tonnes submerged/90·0 m/DE/12 k surface and 17 k submerged. Armed with eight standard 533-mm homing torpedo tubes—six at the bow and two at the stern. **h** US vessel with facilities for carrying amphibious warfare equipment. **i** USSR submarine with above deck missile tanks.

Fig. 139 Nuclear-powered Fleet submarine HMS *Dreadnought* *Crown copyright*

Fig. 140 HMS *Chawton* a 'Ton' class coastal minesweeper in Aberdeen harbour after having arrested a Russian seine netter while on Fishery Protection duties

Mine Warfare Ships

During hostilities minesweeping is often carried out by different types of vessel temporarily fitted for the purpose; many well-known paddle steamers were used in both world wars. Specially built ships are now classified into three groups: ocean, coastal and inshore. Within the general heading of mine warfare ships are *minelayers*, whose function is to lay mines in enemy waters; *mine-hunters*, fitted with sonar mine-hunting equipment capable of locating and classifying mines on the sea-bed from a distance; *minesweepers*, equipped with mine-destroying gear for sweeping contact mines from the surface. The *contact* mine is moored to the sea-bed and floats just below the surface of the sea, exploding on contact with a vessel. It is cleared by long sweepers which are towed on each quarter by the minesweeper, so that the mine can be cut from its mooring. The *magnetic* mine lies on the sea-bed and is activated by the proximity of a ship's steel hull. It must be discovered and detonated by electrical means at a safe distance. The *acoustic* mine also lies on the sea-bed and is activated by the vibrations of a nearby ship's propeller or engines; it must be destroyed by acoustical means. For obvious reasons the minesweeper must have as small a magnetic field as possible; for this reason the smaller vessels have wooden hulls and a good deal of aluminium in their structure. Some ships even have non-magnetic engines, and in recent years fibre-glass and reinforced plastic have been used. Most navies have reduced their numbers of mine-layers and some have no vessels of this type at all now. For both laying and sweeping of mines, aircraft are playing an increasing part in mine warfare.

Mine Warfare Ships

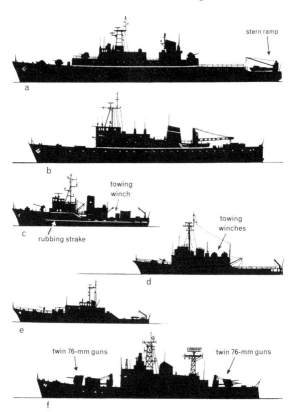

Fig. 141   Mine warfare ships

Fig. 142 Swedish minelayer cum depot ship. *Älvsborg*

By courtesy of the Swedish Naval Attaché

a Swedish Minelayer and Submarine Depot Ship *Älvsborg* class 1971/2,650 tonnes/92·4 m/M/15 k. A dual-purpose vessel with accommodation for 200 men in addition to the crew. On the stern ramp are several minelaying rails running parallel over the low counter. **b** British Mine Counter-measure support ship and minelayer HMS *Abdiel* 1967/1,375 tonnes/80·7 m/M/16 k. Designed to serve a group of minesweepers away from their home base and equipped to carry 44 mines for exercises with these sweepers. **c** British 'Ton' class coastal minesweeper and minehunter. 1953–1960/360 tonnes/46·6 m/M/15 k. A large group of ships used as sweepers, Fishery Protection vessels and headquarters for each of eleven units of the Royal Naval Reserve. Hulls of mahogany and aluminium alloy to reduce magnetic attraction. Some ships fitted with sonar minehunting devices. **d** Ocean minesweeper US *Agile* class 1950s/665 tonnes/52·42 m/M/15 k. Wooden hulls, some non-magnetic engine room and other equipment. **e** French *Circe* class minehunters 1971–3/460 tonnes/46·3 m/M/15 k. The French Navy also has a large number of ocean and coastal mine-sweepers similar to the British 'Ton' class and some ex-United States classes. **f** Danish Mine-layer *Falster* class 1963–4/1,900 tonnes/77 m/M/17 k. Strengthened for ice navigation, she is equipped with two twin mountings of 76-mm guns.

Depot Ships

In appearance, the naval depot ship resembles a large merchantman with high topsides, many portholes and a number of heavy derricks or deck cranes, except that she is painted grey. Her function is to serve as a 'mother' ship to a group of particular warships such as submarines, destroyers or coastal craft. The depot ship is well equipped with workshops and all the materials required for servicing the relevant warships. In addition she may have accommodation, catering and recreational facilities, a chapel, hospital with operating theatre, and a dental surgery. In the US Navy the term 'tender' is used. In recent years tenders for nuclear-powered fleet ballistic missile submarines have been familiar at the US base in the Holy Loch in Scotland.

---

a HMS *Triumph* 1946—converted 1965/13,500 tonnes/213·1 m/ST/14+ k. Converted from wartime *Colossus* class light carrier. She can be distinguished from a carrier by the additions on the ex-flight deck. **b** HMS *Defiance* (ex-*Forth*) 1939 and converted 1966/10,000 tonnes/161·8 m/ST/16 k. Now acts as a support and depot ship for nuclear-powered submarines. **c** USS *Canopus* 1964/21,450 tonnes/196·0 m/ST/18 k. Fleet Ballistic Missile Submarine tender—familiar in British waters (see above). Facilities for accommodating three submarines at any one time. **d** USSR *Ugra* class nuclear submarine support ship. 1961+/6,750 tonnes/138·0 m/M/17. Heavier armament than is usual for a depot ship—eight 57-mm guns in twin mounts. **e** Australian Destroyer Tender *Stalwart* 1968/10,000 tonnes/157·1 m/M/20 k.

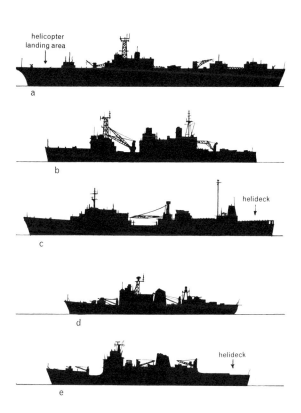

Fig. 143 Depot ships

Fast Patrol Boats

The main characteristics of the fast patrol boat are its small size and its great speed, the latter often in the region of 40 knots. Three main types of craft are built; the *gunboat* armed with a single or twin 40-mm Bofors gun, the *guided missile boat* armed with surface-to-surface missile launchers, and the *torpedo boat* with two or four single 533-mm torpedo tubes. Sometimes craft are designed to be interchangeable, i.e. torpedo or gunboats. The British firm of Vosper Thornycroft, of Southampton, has specialized in the design and construction of fast patrol boats and many of the world's navies possess boats from its yards.

Fig. 144 Malaysian fast patrol boat 1960s/96 tonnes/31·39 m/M/27 k. Vosper Thornycroft

The Royal Navy 'Brave' class boats, from the same yards, are propelled by gas turbines giving a maximum speed of 52 knots, and armed with two Bofors guns and two standard single torpedo tubes. The US Navy possesses several classes of 40-knot boats (some of them propelled by CODOG systems and armed with missile launchers) and a number of hydrofoil boats with a new type of gas turbine propulsion in which the propeller is replaced by rearward water jets. The Russian missile boats are capable of firing surface-to-surface missiles with a range of 18 miles. The hoods over the launchers are distinctive features of the silhouette **b**.

helicopter
landing deck

Fig. 145   HMS *Hecla* class 1965–6/
2,898 gt/79·3 m/DE/14 k maximum

Survey Ships

For many years the Admiralty has been responsible
for the production of world-wide navigation charts
and sailing directions.   For this purpose the Royal
Navy—and similarly other navies—operates a
number of specially designed survey ships.   In
the past some of the ships had other functions as
well, but the latest examples are used solely for
oceanographical and hydrographical work.   The
survey ship must have a long cruising range and be
strengthened against ice.   **Fig. 145** shows a class
of British survey ship which is very well equipped
with drawing offices, chart room, laboratories,
workshops, library, cinema and hospital.   She also,
like so many contemporary warships and auxiliaries, has a helicopter landing deck.

The latest United States survey ships are similar
vessels with a distinctive motor yacht appearance.
They have an extensive cruising range of between
10,000 and 15,000 nautical miles, and in order to
increase their manoeuvrability they are fitted with a
bow thruster unit and controllable pitch propeller.
The newest French survey ship has a rather
different appearance from those described above
as she has a slightly boxlike general appearance,
and the superstructure three-quarters aft.

Fig. 146 Maintenance Ship HMS *Hartland Point*
1945/8,580 tonnes/134·6 m/TE/10 k. The survivor of a group of ships built during the last war,
she resembles a cargo liner in appearance with
many additional deckhouses and heavy cranes.
The function of this type of vessel is practically
the same as the depot ship, as she also has extensive repair and maintenance workshops and
accommodation. This vessel served for a time in
the Far East as a destroyer and frigate depot ship,
and later as an accommodation ship in Belfast.
The French Navy has converted three passenger
liners, and many other navies use ex-merchant
ships for this purpose. The *Hartland Point* is
unusual these days as she is propelled by triple
expansion reciprocating engines.

Fig. 147 Mooring salvage
and boom vessel

This specialized type
of auxiliary is required
for the handling of
heavy moorings and
for maintaining
the net booms

boom gallows
and sheaves

and gates provided in wartime for the protection
of warships against torpedo attack. The easily
recognized feature is the pair of horns projecting
over the bows to which the moorings or buoys can
be lifted. Another feature is the large derrick
forward of the foremast and, although not always
visible, the craft usually has a powerful towing
winch. The more modern ships are motor
vessels capable of a wide range of activities
connected with mooring and boom work.

Fleet Auxiliaries

Ships of the Royal Fleet Auxiliary Service (RFA) play an important role in maintaining the efficiency of fighting ships in peace and in war; they carry oil, fuel, dry cargo, spare parts and many thousands of miscellaneous, but essential, items. They are fitted with varied specialized equipment for supplying RN ships in harbour and at sea, well away from their home ports. In general the ships are similar in appearance to commercial cargo carriers with cargo-handling gear, but much more deck clutter, and they are manned by officers and ratings of the Merchant Navy. Recently helicopters have made a very useful contribution to the work of these support ships and most of the latter now have a helideck aft; some have a helicopter hangar as well.

Operation of the helicopters is in the hands of RN officers and ratings. With the exception of a few tankers, ships of the RFA are painted grey overall, with a light grey funnel and a black top. The ships wear the Blue Ensign defaced by a golden anchor (**Fig. 108**). The procedure of replenishing warships at sea requires fast and easily man-oeuvrable servicing vessels. The latter take up a position on a steady course parallel to, and about 35 metres from, the receiving warship and proceed at exactly the same speed. In order to reduce motion, they both steam into the wind, or against the sea, whichever is the stronger. After contact is made by firing a nylon line across the gap, the oil hoses or jackstays can be sent across and the oil or stores transferred, while the two ships keep up the same speed and course.

Logistics Landing Ship

Fig. 148 RFA *Sir Geraint* 1970/3,370 tonnes/ 125·6 m/M/17 k. Reference has been made on pages 56–62 to RO/RO passenger and cargo vessels, and the drawing below shows a military version of this type of ship. One of several such vessels, she is designed to carry over 300 soldiers and their vehicles for combined services landing operations. With the bow ramp and door she is a development of the wartime tank landing craft, but in addition there are drive-through facilities with a stern door and vehicle ramp. Access from

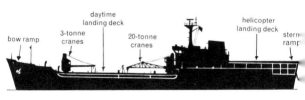

one deck to another is by ramps, and the vessel is equipped with workshops for repair and maintenance of military vehicles. The helicopter landing deck aft of the superstructure can be used at all times during daylight; in calm weather, helicopters can also be landed on the deck amidships, when the deck cranes can be swung out of the way. Armament consists only of a pair of 40-mm Bofors guns for AA defence. Similar ships of a new series have better facilities for loading helicopters on the foredeck. This type of ship can be compared with the US tank landing ships (**Fig. 128d**), although the latter replace the forward bow ramp by a higher one working on projecting derrick arms.

w ramp

open
deck space

Fig. 149   Landing craft

Landing Craft

The logistics landing craft described opposite is designed so that army vehicles can be driven direct from the ship to the beach during a combined forces operation. Any such operation would also need a number of smaller craft, with bow doors, for the same purpose as in the 'D'-Day landings on the north coast of France in June 1944. Earlier in the war this type of landing craft developed from the broad-beamed barge and became a large open-decked vessel with shallow draught and a hinged ramp in the square bows.

Some vessels are as long as 70 metres and carry a large number of troops and vehicles, but the craft built to be carried by assault ships are 24-m vessels with the same characteristics. These new vessels are very seaworthy and are fitted with Kort nozzle rudders (page 16) to ensure better steering and control in shallow waters close to a beach. They are referred to as LCM or Landing Craft Mechanized, as they are capable of transporting either two battle tanks or about 100 tonnes of army vehicles. Some smaller craft in the US Navy are LCVP or Landing Craft Vehicle and Personnel, and experiments are now being made with 30-m air-cushion landing craft with gas turbines and aircraft-type propellers giving a speed of 50 knots. Some of the old war construction tank landing craft have done good service in commercial hands as vehicle ferries—the forerunners of the present-day RO/RO vehicle vessels.

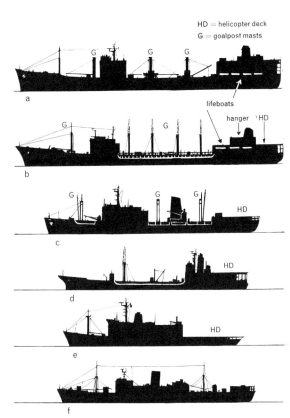

HD = helicopter deck
G = goalpost masts

a

lifeboats

hanger   HD

b

G   G   G   HD

c

HD

d

HD

e

f

Fig. 150 Royal Fleet Auxiliaries

Royal Fleet Auxiliaries

a Replenishment ship *Regent* class 1965/18,029 gt/195·1 m/ST/20 k. Complement composed of 119 RFA crew, 52 civil servants and 11 RN officers and ratings for flying and maintaining the helicopter. The long high poop, with landing deck and hangar, distinguishes the profile from that of a freighter. This is a new purpose-built ship designed to carry dry cargo and ammunition for transfer at sea. **b** Fleet Replenishment Oiler 'Ol' class 1965/22,350 dwt/197·5 m/ST/19 k. This type of supply tanker is distinguished from the commercial tanker by the helideck and the number of heavy goalposts with their jackstays and hose-handling gear. Ships in this class are strengthened against ice; *Olna* has a bow thruster unit. **c** Fleet Support Ship *Lyness* type 1967–8/12,359 gt/159·7 m/M/17 k. This motor logistics ship does not have the usual large hatches of the freighter as they would be too dangerous for underwater transfer of cargoes. She is fitted with goalpost gantries, large deck cranes, and facilities for landing a helicopter. **d** *Rover* class oiler 1970–1/7,060 dwt/140·3 m/M/19 k. A smaller type of oiler than **b**, but designed also to transfer oil fuel, fresh water, dry cargo or stores underway either by helicopter or by the method outlined on page 157. **e** Helicopter Support Ship *Engadine* 1967/6,384 gt/129·2 m/M/16 k. Designed for the training of helicopter crews, this vessel is also equipped for underway replenishment. **f** Store Support ship *Resurgent* 1951 (1954)/9,511 gt/145·3 m/M/15 k. Converted from cargo-passenger liner to carry naval stores.

Fig. 151   The Royal Yacht *Britannia*

The royal yacht *Britannia* was built by John Brown Ltd of Clydebank and was accepted by the Admiralty in January 1954, nine months after she had been launched by Her Majesty the Queen.

The *Britannia* was designed as a dual-purpose vessel: for the peace-time role of conveying members of the royal family to any part of the globe and for the wartime role of naval hospital ship when her stabilizers, special air-conditioning and large laundry would be of special importance. She has two sets of turbines modelled on those made for fast cross-Channel packets giving her a continuous sea speed of 21 knots. She has a gross tonnage of 5,769 and an overall length of 125·5 m. Special attention has been given to the design of the funnel to ensure the minimum interference from smoke and waste gases; the funnel and super-structure above the bridge deck are constructed of aluminium alloy.

The *Britannia*'s royal apartments are placed aft between the main and mizzen masts. Custom demands three masts as when the Sovereign is on board the following flags must be worn: Royal Standard at the main, Lord High Admiral's flag at the fore and Union Flag at the mizzen. The White Ensign is always flown at the stern.

Battleship

Nearly 70 years ago HMS *Dreadnought* revolutionized the design of the battleship and set the pattern for the most important and most powerful units of the world's navies. For more than half a century heavily armoured battleships dominated sea power. Many were equipped with up to ten guns of 14- or 15-inch calibre. The world's largest battleships, built by Japan, even mounted 18-inch guns. Now the battleship's days are over as the development of the guided missile and jet aircraft has rendered the big gun obsolete.

Fig. 152 HMS *Vanguard*

HMS *Vanguard* was the last British battleship. Built in 1946, and scrapped fifteen years later, she spent her last years as HQ ship at Portsmouth. The 35,000-tonne USS *North Carolina*, built in 1937, has been preserved as a war memorial at Wilmington, North Carolina and the *Alabama*, 1942, is similarly preserved at Mobile.

g. 153 Probly the last unds fired by a ttleship. USS *ew Jersey* operng as a fire pport ship off etnam in 1969 *icial US Navy otograph*

Fig. 154
French
frigate
Le Brest

By courtesy
French Nav
Attaché

Fig. 155 Swedish fast patrol boat armed with one 57-mm gun, light missiles and six torpedo tubes

By courtesy of Swedish Naval Attaché

Fig. 156 Helicopter support ship RFA *Engadine*

P. A. Vicary

UNITED STATES CLASSIFICATION OF NAVAL SHIPS AND SERVICE CRAFT

Aircraft Carriers: Attack carrier **CVA**; Nuclear Attack carrier **CVAN**; Support carrier **CVS**. *Surface Combatants:* Battleship **BB**; Heavy cruiser **CA**; Guided missile cruiser **CG**; Nuclear guided missile cruiser **CGN**; Light cruiser **CL**; Guided missile light cruiser **CLG**; Destroyer **DD**; Guided missile destroyer **DDG**; Radar picket destroyer **DDR**; Frigate **DL**; Guided missile frigate **DLG**; Nuclear missile frigate **DLGN**. *Ocean Escorts:* Escort ship **DE**; Guided missile escort ship **DEG**; Radar picket escort ship **DER**. *Command ship* **CC**. *Submarines* **SS**; Nuclear submarine **SSN**; Guided missile submarine **SSG;** Fleet ballistic missile submarine (nuclear) **SSBN.** *Patrol ships* **P.** *Amphibious Warfare Ships:* (selection) Command ship **LCC;** Fire support ship **LFS;** Assault ship **LPH;** Amphibious transport submarine **LPSS;** Dock landing ship **LSD;** Tank landing ship **LST.** *Mine Warfare Ships:* Countermeasure ship **MCS**; Coastal minesweeper (non-magnetic) **MSC**; Fleet minesweeper (steel hull) **MSF**; Ocean minesweeper (non-magnetic) **MSO**. *Combatant Craft:* Patrol craft (hydrofoil) **PCH**; Patrol gunboat (hydrofoil) **PGH**; Fast patrol craft **PTF**. *Landing Craft:* Assault **LCA**; Mechanized **LCM**; Personnel (large) **LCPL**; Personnel (ramped) **LCPR**; Utility **LCU**; Vehicle (personnel) **LCVP**; Warping tug **LWT**. *Mines Countermeasures Craft:* Boat **MSB**; Drone **MSD**; Inshore **MSI**; Launch **MSL**; River **MSM**; Patrol **MSR**; Special (device) **MSS**. *Riverine warfare craft:* various with no common letter. *Auxiliaries* **A**. *Service craft* code begins with **A** or **Y**.

American warships show hull numbers but not type designation letters (cf. page 120).

Fig. 157 Parts of a sailing vessel

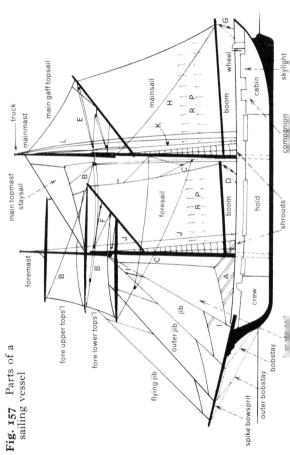

166

6 SAILING SHIPS

PARTS OF A SAILING SHIP
(TOPSAIL SCHOONER)

Rigging

A   Jib and forestaysail sheets
B   Upper and lower topsail braces
C   Fore braces
D   Fore sheet
E   Main peak halliards (or halyards)
F   Fore peak halliards
G   Main sheet
H   Main boom topping lift
I   Forestay
J   Fore topmast backstay
K   Main topmast backstay
L   Signal halliards
RP Reef points

Rigging can be divided into two categories: *standing rigging*, which helps to maintain masts in their permanent positions, and *running rigging*, which controls the movement of yards and sails.

Standing Rigging

A forestay passes from the top of a mast downwards in a forward direction.

A backstay passes from the top of a mast downwards to both sides of the vessel to take the forward strain of the mast.

Shrouds pass from the top of a mast (or a point on it) to the ship's sides.

Ratlines are short lengths of line which cross the shrouds at intervals and form ladders to the upper parts of the masts.

Running Rigging

A lift takes the weight of a yard or boom.

Halliards raise or lower a spar or sail, or may be used for signal flags.

Braces control the fore-and-aft movement of the yards.

Clew lines lift the lower corners of a square sail.

To *bend* a sail is to attach it to a yard or boom, and to *furl* it is to secure it temporarily to a spar by short lengths of line called gaskets. The spike bowsprit has generally taken the place of the more elaborate jib-boom bowsprit. The former consists of one spar only.

The names of the spars, sails and rigging of a large square-rigged vessel follow the same system of nomenclature as shown for the topsail schooner.

These are the names of the sails of a square-rigged mast, starting from deck level: *course, lower-topsail, upper-topsail, lower-topgallant, upper-topgallant, royal* and in some instances *skysail.* Names of masts of a four-mast barque: *fore, main, mizzen* and *jigger.*

In naming a sail the name of the mast comes first, followed by the name of the sail. For example: *fore upper-topsail* refers to the third sail from deck level on the foremast, and *mizzen upper-topgallant* refers to the fifth sail on the third mast of a full-rigged ship or four-masted barque.

The *mizzen-course* is sometimes referred to as the *cro'jack.* Several giant five-mast barques have been built and their fifth masts have been variously called *after-jigger, after spanker* or *pusher.*

Sailing Schoolships

Before the last war a few square-rigged ocean-going ships were employed in the carriage of cargoes, mainly in the Australian grain trade. In the post-war period the German cargo-cadet four-masted barques *Pamir* and *Passat* sailed in this trade, but after the former foundered in a hurricane off the Azores in September 1957, with the loss of 80 lives, the other vessel was laid up. Interest in sail was revived in 1956 with the first of the 'Tall Ships' races from Torbay to Lisbon, established by the Sail Training Association. The opportunity of seeing so many square-rigged and other large sailing vessels together created great excitement, and this has been maintained by the biennial race held on different courses.

Enthusiasts in this country alone have always regretted that Great Britain, almost alone of the seafaring nations, has not possessed a square-rigged sailing schoolship. This disappointment has been rectified to some extent by the building of three three-masted tops'l schooners and a brig, since 1965. Some governments provide, by means of their sailing schoolships, long courses of professional training for boys who wish to take up a career at sea either in the merchant navy or in fighting ships. Most of the sailing schoolships provide shorter courses for boys—or girls—as a part of general education, in the belief that qualities of leadership and the development of character can result. There are about 30 square-rigged sailing schoolships in service and many more fore-and-aft rigged craft serving the same purpose. About 30 more ships and barques are employed as floating schools, or museums. Many of these vessels were originally cargo-carriers built towards the end of the nineteenth century.

Full-rigged Ship

The **full-rigged ship** is a sailing vessel with square sails on all three, or four, masts. This was the rig of many of the fine sailing vessels of the middle nineteenth century when the famous China tea clippers achieved such high speeds and performance. The British ship, *Cutty Sark*, was the most famous of these. Built at Dumbarton in 1869 with a tonnage of 921 gt, and a length of 64·61 m, she made many record passages. After a period as a stationary sail training ship, she is now restored and dry-berthed at Greenwich. The Glasgow-built ship *Balclutha* (1886) has also been restored and remains afloat at the San Francisco Maritime Museum.

Fig. 158
Full-rigged ship

Ship-rigged Schoolships

Based on Kristiansand in South Norway, the *Sørlandet* was built in 1927 with a tonnage of 577 gross and an overall length of 52·42 m. She has accommodation for about 100 cadets. During the last war she was almost completely destroyed. In 1947 she was entirely rebuilt along with the *Christian Radich*, which had capsized during the war and also seemed to be beyond repair. Built in 1937, she is a slightly larger vessel of 676 tons gross and a length of 58·52 m, and has accommo-

Fig. 159
Danish
Schoolship.
Full-rigged
ship *Danmark*

*Skyfotos,
Ashford, Kent*

dation for about the same number of cadets. She is based on Oslo. The Danish *Danmark* of 1933 has a tonnage of 777 tons gross, a length of 57·29 m and can carry rather more cadets than the two Norwegian ships. During the last war she sailed under the United States flag as a training ship for the Coast Guard Service. The *Georg Stage*, also belonging to Denmark, was built in 1935 to replace a ship of the same name which became the *Joseph Conrad* and was run for several years as a privately owned schoolship. The latter is now preserved at Mystic, Connecticut. The present ship—203 tons, 37·48 m can be identified by her black hull. The Polish *Dar Pomorza* is a very much older ship than all these as she was built in 1909 as the *Prinzess Eitel Friedrich* and transferred to Poland in 1930. She has accommodation for between 150 and 200 cadets, and has a length of 72·84 m and 1,566 gross tons. The Italian *Amerigo Vespucci* (1930) and her sister ship *Cristofo Colombo* (1931), which now belongs to Russia, are unusual looking ships with a very high freeboard and hulls which are reminiscent of the early nineteenth-century ships-of-the-line. Argentina's *Libertad* (1958) has a gross tonnage of 3,765 and a full complement of 360 officers, crew and cadets.

Fig. 160 Three-masted barque

Barque

By the end of the nineteenth century the **barque** rig had become popular. It differed from the ship rig in that no square sails were crossed on the mizzen and consequently a smaller crew was required. At this time there was a shortage of crews and many full-rigged ships were converted to barque rig; it was found that they often gained in sailing qualities. In the first decades of this century the sailing ship rapidly declined in numbers. Between the wars a shipowner from the Baltic Åland Islands bought a number of the barques and operated them in the Australian grain trade—undermanned and uninsured. Some of these merchant vessels carried cadets, but they were not sail training ships in the true sense.

Barque-rigged Schoolships

The most modern craft of this rig is the West German *Gorch Fock* of 1,870 tonnes displacement, built in 1959 to carry 140 cadets. She has a long poop and the characteristic German double spanker gaffs instead of the normal single spanker. The Norwegian 1,710 tonne barque *Statsraad Lehmkuhl*, built in 1914 as the *Grossherzog Friedrich August*, is based at Bergen. Perhaps the best known of all the sail training vessels is the American *Eagle* built in Germany in 1936 as the *Horst Wessel*, 1,634 tonnes displacement and a length of 80·72 m, and taken over at the end of the war by the United States Coast Guard Service. One of her sister ships, *Gorch Fock*, passed to the Russians at the same time and was renamed *Tovarisch*, while yet another sister, the *Albert Leo Schlageter* became the Brazilian *Guanabara* and now sails as the Portuguese *Sagres*. Russia also possesses two other sail training barques: *Krusenstern* (ex *Padua*) built in 1926 and *Sedov* (ex-*Kommodore Johnsen* ex *Magdalene Vinnen*). Two large schoolships belonging to Japan are the four-masted barques *Nippon Maru* (1930) and *Kaiwo Maru* (1931). These large sister ships each have a tonnage of 2,284 and a length of 79·2 m but, with rather high freeboard, a navigating bridge and a small funnel they are less attractive than the more traditional sailers. A few other barques are in use as stationary schoolships in various ports with no prospect of going to sea again.

Fig. 161 Barque *Christian Radich*

Barquentine *Regina Maris*

Brig

The **brig** is a two-mast sailing vessel with square sails on each mast and fore-and-aft staysails, jibs and a spanker.   This was a common rig for coastal and short-sea traders of the last century, and the well-known East-coast colliers were usually rigged in this way.   Some of the fastest brigs of the period were the fish carriers, bringing cod from the New-foundland Banks to Bristol and other ports.   The

Fig. 162   Brig

snow was similar to the brig except that the span-ker was set on a trysail-mast just abaft the main lower mast, which extended from the deck to the main top.   Later the term referred to either a snow, or brig rigged vessel from the Baltic. During the nineteenth century the Royal Navy continued to use both brigs and snows as training ships long after steamships had become firmly established in the fleet.

In 1971 the brig *Royalist* was launched for the Sea Cadet Corps.   She has accommodation for 20 boys training for careers in the Royal Navy, or the Merchant Navy, and goes on short cruises throughout the year from her base at Whale

Island, Portsmouth. Her 'period' look, with painted square ports and stern boat davits, ensures that she is easily identified.

Fig. 163
British Schoolship. Brig *Royalist*

Skyfotos, Ashford, Kent

Brigantine

The **brigantine** has two masts, the foremast fully square-rigged and the mainmast with gaff mainsail and staysails. This rig was earlier known as the **hermaphrodite** *brig*, as the real brig had square topsails on the main topmast, but the term soon dropped out of use. The only brigantine rigged schoolship is the 200-ton *Wilhelm Pieck* built in 1951 for the training of merchant seaman in Eastern Germany. Although classified as a brigantine, she has a gaff foresail and a slightly different arrangement of her square sails.

Fig. 164
Brigantine

Barquentine

The **barquentine** is a three-mast vessel with square sails on the foremast, staysails between the fore and main masts, and gaff sails and gaff topsails on the main and mizzen masts. This type evolved in order to reduce running costs; fore and aft sails require less manpower than square sails. The schoolship *Mercator*, owned by the Belgian government, is a good example of the barquentine. Built at Leith in 1932, she was originally rigged as a topsail schooner but was later re-rigged as a barquentine. The Indonesian *Dewarutji* is a similar vessel built in Germany in 1952 to accommodate 78 cadets and a crew of 32. The Brazilian *Almirante Saldanha* is a four-mast barquentine built in 1933 as a sail training ship and now employed

Fig. 165
Barquentine

in oceanographic survey; with her high freeboard, large number of portholes and engine exhausts, she is a hybrid. A former Portuguese Grand Banks fishing vessel, the barquentine *Gazela Primeriro* is now preserved in Philadelphia, USA. In 1972 a barquentine was to be seen in the English Channel area. She was the 400-ton Swedish built *Eolus*, converted from schooner rig in 1970 for charter cruise work in the South Pacific. The 188-ton barquentine *Regina Maris* (page 173), now stationed at Los Angeles for a similar purpose, was previously seen in European waters.

176

Fig. 166

Juan Sebastian de Elcano

Topsail schooner

The **topsail schooner** is a fore-and-aft rigged sailing vessel with one or more square sails set on the foremast; it is the commonest rig of the smaller present-day schoolship. The largest likely to be seen in European waters is the Spanish *Juan Sebastian de Elcano*, launched in Spain in 1927 (designed in Great Britain), with a length of 93·83 m and a displacement tonnage of 3,222. She has a long poop, several deckhouses, boats and other gear between the forecastle and poop. Her near sister, but barquentine-rigged ship, built about the same time, became the Chilean *Esmeralda*, which normally operates in the Pacific.

The Yugoslavian three-mast schooner *Jadran* is a smaller vessel with a length of 57·91 m. She has a long forecastle and a long poop linked together by a shelter deck; she was built in 1931 with accommodation for 150 cadets and their instructors. In Great Britain there are now four tops'l sail training schooners. In 1955 the Outward Bound Moray Sea School, Burghead, acquired and converted the Danish *Peder Most* (1944) and renamed her *Prince Louis* to replace an earlier vessel of the same name. The Sail Training Association now owns two three-mast schooners: the *Sir Winston Churchill* (1965) and her sister *Malcolm Miller*. Each of these has accommodation for 34 boys or girls, and a crew of nine men.

Fig. 167

Sir Winston Churchill

The latest British schoolship with this rig is the *Captain Scott*, built in 1971 for the Dulverton Trust and based on the West coast of Scotland at Plockton. She operates four-week cruises, with 36 young people aboard, on combined sailing and mountaineering adventure courses. She has a length of 43·89 m and a tonnage slightly larger than the two STA schooners. Two pairs of tops'l schooners are now familiar in European waters. The French Government two-mast tops'l schooners *La Belle-Poule* and *L'Etoile*, built in 1932, cross two yards on the foremast with roller reefing gear for the topsail. They are modelled on the small Breton schooners or *terre neuvas* of the Newfoundland cod fisheries. The two Swedish schooners, *Gladan* and *Falken*, are 214-ton vessels built in 1947. They can be differentiated from the French pair by their single yards and running square sail, as well as the gaff fore topsail in place of the French vessels' main topmast staysail.

For many years Lord Runciman's famous yacht the three-mast topsail schooner *Sunbeam II* was well known in her original role, and later as the Swedish sail training vessel *Flying Clipper*. This schooner is now the Greek *Eugene Eugenides*.

In the last century, but in rapidly diminishing numbers during this one, the trading schooner was very common around British shores. No vessel now exists in trade but, fortunately, two of the last vessels have been preserved. The Maritime Trust has the last British wooden trading schooner, *Kathleen and May* (1900), on view at the Barbican, Plymouth; the last actual trading schooner, *Result* (1893)—until recently a two-mast auxiliary sailing vessel—has been acquired for preservation by the Ulster Folk Museum.

Fig. 168
Kathleen and May (1900)

Fig. 169
Result: original rig of 1893

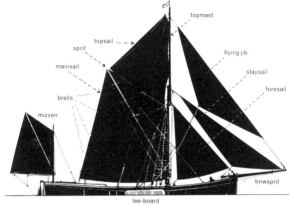

topmast

topsail

sprit

mainsail

flying jib

staysail

foresail

brails

mizzen

lee-board

bowsprit

Fig. 170

Thames spritsail barge

Sailing Barge

In the early part of this century about 2,000 sailing barges traded in the Thames estuary and along the South and East coasts. By the end of the 1950s about 80 sailed without auxiliary power, and this number has now dwindled away to one or two barges trading, or on charter. Interest in this attractive survival of sail is, however, retained when most of the 20 or so survivors—mainly as private yachts—take part in the Pin Mill, Blackwater and Medway annual sailing barge races.

The characteristic feature of the barge is the huge mainsail supported by a 15–18 metre sprit. For furling, this sail is gathered up to the mast by means of brails. This feature, and others, enable the craft to be sailed by only two men. Not all barges have a bowsprit and some have a gaff and boom 'mule rigged' mizzen. Both masts are set in tabernacles so that they can be lowered for the negotiation of low bridges.

7 GENERAL INFORMATION Part II

Abbreviations

A foremost gun turret; **AA** anti-aircraft; **AS** anti-submarine; **ASDIC** Allied Submarine Detection Investigation Committee; **B** second gun turret from bows; **bhp** brake horse power; **bp** between perpendiculars; **CODOG** combined diesel/gas turbine propulsion; **COGOG** full gas turbine propulsion; **COSAG** combined steam/gas turbines; **CSD** closed shelter deck; **DE** diesel-electric; **DF** direction finder; **DP** dual-purpose; **d.w.** or **dwt** deadweight tonnage; **FPB** fast patrol boat; **FV** fishing vessel; **GP** general purpose; **gt** or **g.r.t.** gross registered tonnage; **GT** gas turbine; **HA/LA** high angle/low angle; **HMAS** Her Majesty's Australian Ship; **HMNZS** Her Majesty's New Zealand Ship; **HMS** Her Majesty's Ship; **HWOST** high water ordinary spring tides; **k** knot; **LASH** Lighter aboard ship vessel; **LPG** liquefied propane gas carrier; **LR** Lloyd's Register; **LWOST** low water ordinary spring tides; **MN** Merchant Navy; **MTB** motor torpedo boat; **MV** merchant ship or motor vessel; **NAC** Naval Air Command; **n.r.t** net registered tonnage; **o.a.** length overall; **OBO** oil/bulk/ore carrier; **OSD** open shelter deck; **PS** paddle steamer; **RFA** Royal Fleet Auxiliary; **RM** Royal Marines; **RMS** Royal Mail Ship; **RN** Royal Navy; **RNLI** Royal National Lifeboat Institution; **RNR** Royal Naval Reserve; **RO/RO** roll on/roll off; **s.h.p.** shaft horse power; **SOS** radiotelegraph distress signal; **SR** steam reciprocating engines; **TE** turbo electric; **SS** steamship; **TSS** turbine steamship; **USS** United States Ship; **VLCC** very large crude oil carrier; **wl** water-line; **WT** wireless telegraphy; **X** gun turret forward of the aftermost one; **Y** aftermost gun turret.

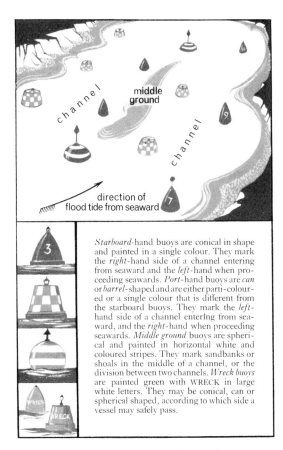

Starboard-hand buoys are conical in shape and painted in a single colour. They mark the *right*-hand side of a channel entering from seaward and the *left*-hand when proceeding seawards. *Port*-hand buoys are *can* or *barrel*-shaped and are either parti-coloured or a single colour that is different from the starboard buoys. They mark the *left*-hand side of a channel entering from seaward, and the *right*-hand when proceeding seawards. *Middle ground* buoys are spherical and painted in horizontal white and coloured stripes. They mark sandbanks or shoals in the middle of a channel, or the division between two channels. *Wreck buoys* are painted green with WRECK in large white letters. They may be conical, can or spherical shaped, according to which side a vessel may safely pass.

Fig. 171 Buoyage System of the United Kingdom

Anchor or riding lights. An all-round white light on the forestay 6 to 12 metres above the hull and, at the stern, a similar white light 4.5 metres lower than the forward light.

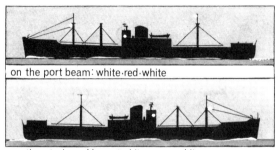

on the port beam: white · red · white

on the starboard beam: white · green · white

from starboard bow   right ahead   on the port bow

Steaming lights. A white light on the foremast 6 to 12 metres above the hull visible ahead and two points ($22\frac{1}{2}°$) abaft either beam; a similar white light on the mainmast at least 4.5 metres higher than the forward light. *Side or bow lights,* placed lower than the white lights and visible right ahead and two points abaft the beam, *red* on the *port* side and *green* on the *starboard* side. A white *stern light* is shown by a vessel when being overtaken.

Fig. 172 Navigation Lights for vessels over 45 metres in length

Glossary

Armour belt Band of protective steel plating on sides of a warship's water-line. **Ballast** Heavy material carried to ensure stability—usually water. **In Ballast** Sailing without cargo. **Berth** Loading or discharging position at a quay. **Bilge keel** Longitudinal external keel at turn of the hull to resist rolling and improve steering. **Binnacle** Free-standing mounting for compass. **Bitts** Pair of strong steel columns for mooring ropes. **Bollard** Single steel post on ship or quayside for mooring ropes. **Boot-topping** Area of a ship's hull roughly between the light and loaded water-lines painted a distinctive colour. **Bow thruster** Small propeller in an athwartships tunnel near a ship's stem to increase manoeuvrability at slow speeds. **Bridge deck** Superstructure containing navigating bridge, wheelhouse, chart room and captain's quarters. **Bulbous bow** Rounded projection of the ship's forefoot to reduce resistance when in ballast. **Bulkhead** Vertical transverse or longitudinal steel partition in a ship's hull. **Bulwark** 1-metre high steel plating along the side of the deck for safety of crew or passengers. **Bunker** Space for storing fuel. **Bunkers** The fuel itself. **Capstan** Upright revolving pillar for manipulating mooring or other ropes. **Catwalk** Light connecting bridge. **Coaming** Raised lip of plating round the edge of a hatchway. **Cofferdam** Double watertight bulkheads. **Companion** Ladder or staircase connecting two decks. **Conning tower** Part of a warship's bridge and the superstructure of a submarine. **Cowl** Upper part of a ventilator or smoke baffle on a funnel. **Crosstrees** Small platform at the head of a lower mast. **Davit** Radial, quadrant or gravity type fitting for support and lowering of lifeboats. **Deadlight**

Watertight steel shutter to protect scuttle or port-hole. **Derrick** Swinging spar for lifting and slewing cargo. **Draught** Depth of water necessary to float a ship. **Entrance** Tapering part of hull between parallel sides and pointed stem. **Fairlead** Short vertical deck fittings for guidance of ropes. **Fender** Rope, rubber or cane pad to protect ship's side. **Flotsam** Floating goods lost by shipwreck or thrown overboard. **Forecastle** or **Fo'c'sle** Raised forward part of a ship's hull. **Freeboard** Distance between water-line and main deck. **Freighter** American term for a cargo ship. **Gaff** Spar at head of a fore-and-aft sail or similar diagonal spar for flags. **Galley** Ship's kitchen. **Gallows** Inverted U-shaped fitting at side of a fishing boat's deck. **Guided missile** Rocket type weapon. **Gunhouse** Lightly protected house on gun mounting. **Gunshield** Frontal protection for gun crew. **Gunwale** Upper edge of a boat's side. **Hance** or **fishplate** Curved plating between change of level of ship's bulwarks. **Hatchway** Opening in a deck with a movable cover, i.e. a **hatch. Hawespipe** Steel tube between forecastle deck and ship's side through which anchor cable passes. **Helideck** Landing platform for helicopter. **Helm** Mechanism for operating ship or boat's rudder. **Hogging** Strain on a vessel's hull when, with the crest of a wave amidships, the ends tend to droop. **Island** Raised part of ship's hull. **Jetsam** Goods thrown overboard to lighten ship and washed up ashore. **Keel** Centre longitudinal box girder forming vessel's backbone. **Keelson** or **kelson** Fore-and-aft girder connecting ship's floor to the keel. **Kingpost** or **Sampson post** Post supporting derricks, usually in pairs and sometimes incorporating ventilators. **Goalpost masts** if pair joined by a horizontal bar. **Limbo** Mortar type depth-charge thrower. **Liner** Passenger or cargo vessel on regular service between ports. **Mack** Combined funnel and mast. **Magazine** Space for storing ammunition. **Mizzen** Third mast from bows or fishing vessel's aftermost mast. **Monkey Island** Platform above wheelhouse with extra binnacle. **Orlop** Lowermost deck of a warship or part deck which is not continuous. **Periscope** Long tube with arrangement of mirrors to enable submarine's officers to con surface of the sea while submerged. **Poop** Raised part of hull at the stern. **Porthole** Circular glazed 'window' in ship's side or superstructure plating. **Propeller** or **screw** Spiral blade driving mechanism. **Quarter deck** Aftermost deck of a warship or sailing ship reserved for officers or deck raised about half the normal height. **Radar** Electronic device for 'seeing' at night or in fog (*r*adio *d*etection *a*nd *r*anging). **Radome** Spherical protective shield for radar scanner. **Rudder** Flat vertical steering plate at ship's stern —sometimes additional rudder at the bows. **Run** Tapering part of ship's hull between parallel body and the stern. **Rubbing strake** Additional external length of wood running almost length of ship's sides to protect the hull from damage by quay-wall. **Sagging** Effect on hull when wave crests are at each end. **Seacat** Close range guided missile system for air defence. **Seaslug** Medium range missile system. **Seebee** Barge carrying vessel similar to LASH. **Screw** Propeller. **Scuttle** Glazed opening in hull or superstructure, or to sink a ship deliberately. **Scuppers** Openings to give deck drainage. **Sheerstrake** Uppermost line of plates on ship's side sometimes rounded at deck level. **Shelter deck** Deck above main deck usually with tonnage opening. **Soft-nosed stem** Rounded above water-line—often with company's emblem or badge. **Snort** Tube by which air is drawn into submarine while submerged. **Sonar** *So*und *N*avigation *A*nd *R*anging —underwater searching device like ASDIC. **Spanker** or driver, fore-and-aft gaff sail on aftermost mast of a sailing ship. **Spirket plate** Short section of bulwark on each side of forecastle at the stem. **Squid** Earlier type of mortar depth-charge thrower. **Stabilizers** Movable horizontal fins which can project from a ship's underwater hull to minimize rolling. **Stack** American term for funnel. **Stem** Foremost part of a ship's hull. **Stern** Aftermost part of the hull. **Stern tube** Long watertight steel tube in which the propeller shaft runs. **Strongback** Steel transverse hoop over a tug's after deck to protect deck fittings from tow rope. **Superstructure** Bridge, decks and deckhouses rising above ship's main structure—as distinct from islands which are part of it. **Topsides** Sides of hull between boot-topping and shelter deck level. **Tramp** A cargo vessel engaged in casual trade or on charter—not part of a regular service. **Triatic stay** Wire stay passing from truck of one mast to another. **Truck** Circular wooden cap at head of a mast with sheaves through which the signal halyards pass. **Turret** Totally enclosed and armoured rotating housing for one or more guns. **Turtleback** Forecastle with strongly curved sheerstrakes. **Tweendeck** Additional decks below main deck. **Wash ports** Freeing ports at foot of bulwarks for escape of excessive water. **Whaleback** Turtle-back forecastle of a fishing boat with working space beneath. **Well deck** Deck between two islands. **Winch** Steam, electric or hydraulic deck machinery for hoisting or hauling. **Windlass** Similar machine for hauling in anchor cable on forecastle.

INDEX OF SHIP TYPES

INDEX OF SHIP NAMES AND CLASS DESIGNATIONS